I0804042

Continuing the Journey

Continuing the Journey is a five-book series on advanced approaches to teaching English language arts. Written for veteran teachers by Leila Christenbury and Ken Lindblom, the books include "From the Teachers' Lounge," an innovative feature that honors the expertise of both colleagues from the field and highly regarded scholars. Topics addressed in the series include literature and informational texts; language and writing; listening, speaking, and presenting; digital literacies; and living the professional life of a veteran teacher.

Continuing the Journey

Becoming a Better Teacher of Literature and Informational Texts

Leila Christenbury

Virginia Commonwealth University

Ken Lindblom

Stony Brook University, State University of New York

NCTE National Council of Teachers of English

1111 W. Kenyon Road, Urbana, Illinois 61801-1096

Figures 5.1 and Table 5.1 reprinted from *Supporting Students in a Time of Core Standards: English Language Arts, Grades 9–12* by Sarah Brown Wessling with Danielle Lillge and Crystal VanKooten. © 2011 by NCTE. Reprinted with permission.

Staff Editor: Bonny Graham

Interior Design: Ashlee Goodwin

Cover Design: Pat Mayer

NCTE Stock Number: 08543; eStock Number: 08550
ISBN 978-0-8141-0854-3; eISBN 978-0-8141-0855-0

For the full Library of Congress Cataloging-in-Publication Data for this book, go to www.loc.gov and search for LCCN 2017043132.

To Hollis, my beloved sister, who, as a teacher,
gave her students both her expertise and her joy.

—Leila

To my many teaching colleagues at Columbia High School,
Syracuse University, Madison-Oneida BOCES, Illinois State University,
Stony Brook University, and the thousands of others I've worked with
in school district partnerships or at professional conferences.
We're all in this together!

—Ken

CONTENTS

Acknowledgments

As teachers we work in community, and much of what we learn is by example and through apprenticeship. Little that we do that is successful is independent of others who are both companions on the journey and lead the way. The writing of this book would not have been possible without the many teachers whose voices are represented here. For their contributions in our Teachers' Lounge, in our veteran teacher commentaries, or in other parts of this text, we gratefully acknowledge and thank the following: Victoria Alessi, Deborah Alvarez, Katherine Byers, Clary W. Carleton, Amy E. Harter Casey, Jocelyn A. Chadwick, Alex Corbitt, Lisa Storm Fink, Nicole Galante, Kelly Gallagher, Kara Greenwood, Marie Gist, Doug Hesse, Sharon Hinkson, Susan Houser, Lauren Leigh Kelly, Penny Kittle, Jennifer Menzel, Sarah L. Morris, Thomas Newkirk, Kelly Ann Pace, R. Joseph Rodriguez, Anna J. Small Roseboro, Lisa Scherff, Amy Jo Southworth, Sierra Ware, and Sarah Brown Wessling. We also thank Kevin Cannon, who composed the caricatures of Ken and Leila, which we hope will enliven the pages of this text.

We also appreciate the confidence and support of the National Council of Teachers of English (NCTE). The enthusiasm of NCTE Executive Director Emily Kirkpatrick has been truly sustaining, and we are delighted she agreed to author a foreword. We also thank NCTE Publications Director Kurt Austin for his good advice and steadfast work, and Bonny Graham for her excellent editing skills. Anonymous NCTE reviewers gave us insightful comments and suggestions on the manuscript, and we thank them for their generous and specific feedback. For both of us, Ken and Leila, NCTE is our professional home, and we are honored to have this book published by the organization.

Finally, as not just writers and teachers but as fallible and occasionally grumpy humans, we thank those around us at home. For Leila, it is Tucker, who is both grounded and grounding—much love to you, Techno Man extraordinaire. For Ken, it is Patty, whose companionship—often in the form of mandatory walks, smoothies, and ukulele concerts—completely nourishes him. For both of us, our debt is huge, and we try to repay it every day.

Foreword

EMILY KIRKPATRICK
EXECUTIVE DIRECTOR, NATIONAL COUNCIL OF TEACHERS OF ENGLISH

Renewal. Such is the season within NCTE at the time of conceiving this book series and its first publication. As we Turn the Page on many things within the professional organization for English teachers, a foundational turn is to reclaim the English classroom as the very center of our universe. We renew our energy toward supporting and leading the mainstay of every classroom, too—and that is the English teacher.

In a conversation between the three of us, Leila and Ken's idea for this book series intersected with NCTE's exploration of new ways to spur renewal within the profession. Producing this flagship first book—and envisioning all that is yet to come—is indeed a continuous journey. We welcome the esteemed authors home to NCTE, and also embrace their wisdom, experiences, and strategies for continuous improvement.

I see NCTE as the nexus of practice and progress in English and literacy education. True to that form, the authors have wisely involved nearly two dozen accomplished teachers—and NCTE members—to add to the formative insight included in the following pages. As you turn the pages of this book and the forthcoming series installments, we encourage you to turn and return to the Teachers' Lounge for ongoing ideas, problem solving, and comfort.

Continued journeys are naturally filled with opportunities for continuous improvement. This series is designed to support that, with the scaffolding of trusted leaders Leila and Ken and their treasure trove of friends and colleagues found in the innovative Teachers'

Lounge. Each reader and future reader is invited to Turn the Page with NCTE as we continue to unfold the mysteries and practices destined to guide the next generation of readers and writers in our world.

CHAPTER 1

Changes in You, Changes in Your Classroom, Changes in Your School

And do not think of the fruit of action . . .
Not fare well,
But fare forward, voyagers.

—T.S. Eliot, The Dry Salvages,
Four Quartets (III, 38, 46–47)

What is a veteran teacher?

New teachers are nervous about new teacher things: Will the students listen to me? Can I develop an authoritative classroom presence? What do I say if a parent calls? Will I always be just one day ahead of the students on the reading? Will I do well on my formal observations? What happens if I make a mistake in front of the students or if I don't know an answer to their questions? Will I react appropriately if an emergency occurs in my class?

Veteran teachers are past most of those concerns, except for occasional hiccups. But that doesn't mean they are done becoming better teachers.

It means they are ready to focus entirely on the real challenge of teaching: doing everything necessary to ensure that all students learn as quickly and as much as possible. This deceptively simple task is fraught with complexity. Students' ability levels, backgrounds, prior learning and experience in and out of school, home lives, attitudes, and personal preferences all make a difference in the ability to learn. School cultures, leadership, the standards of the state and/or school system, and the local politics of schooling and evaluation of teachers also make a difference. The world outside school, including leaps in technology and disciplinary content, changes in national and global culture, and state and national education policies, makes a difference. Add to all this the fact that about 13 percent of the teaching force (or 457,000 teachers) changes schools or leaves the profession every year (Haynes). Veteran teachers know teaching is not a profession for the faint of heart!

Who is this book for?

There are lots of good books for beginning teachers, and we humbly suggest that our recently published *Making the Journey: Being and Becoming a Teacher of English Language Arts* (Christenbury and Lindblom, 4th ed.) might be counted among them. But it takes three to seven years for a teacher to become highly skilled (Haynes 5), and even those teaching for more years than that continue to face new challenges and are eager to learn about new pedagogical methods, technologies, and content that will enrich their classrooms. Veteran teachers can use guidance, too. Some districts—but not nearly enough—have excellent mentoring and induction programs that work with teachers beyond their first years in the classroom. But what about the teachers who don't have access to those programs? Those are the teachers to whom we offer this book, the first in a series of books planned with the National Council of Teachers of English (NCTE). This Continuing the Journey series is written primarily for teachers in approximately years 3–10 and those who support them (mentors, senior colleagues, department chairs, and school leaders). These are veteran teachers who can manage a classroom, speak authoritatively with parents, and approach new content with confidence. If this is you, then in many ways you are in the perfect position to take your ELA teaching to the highest levels. And we are honored to assist you in making that climb.

How does one start taking the next step, continuing the journey to becoming a more skilled veteran teacher? We suggest that, like the world's greatest explorers, you begin by surveying the territory: where you've come from and where you're going.

WHEN YOU FIRST STARTED TEACHING

Who were you when you first started teaching? If your life were a film, could you rewind it to see yourself back then, to recapture for a moment the person you were? At the time, what did you believe and what did you trust? What did you think the future would hold?

When you first started teaching, you were likely a person with a strong set of beliefs, goals, and ideals, much of which came from two sources.

First, you had behind you years of being a successful student and observing and participating in numerous classes and with numerous teachers. Second, at the point when you decided to be a teacher, you completed some form of a teacher preparation program that gave you information about school curricula, learning, and how to connect with your students. These two sources were probably much of the foundation for the beginning of your teaching career. And, at the time you entered your first classroom, you may well have thought that most of your struggles were largely in the past; after all, you were starting your career and had cleared academic and credentialing hurdles, you had a contract with a school system, and, if you were lucky, you had, at the beginning of the year, your own classroom, supportive colleagues, and helpful materials to guide you in your teaching. All clear and all set, right?

Not so much.

Like many of us who are still teaching, what you most likely realized early on is that you were not *clear* and not *set* at all. The beliefs, goals, and ideals with which you started began to shift and evolve, and the recollection of your time as a student has become far less reliable as an indication of what you should do as a teacher. The students you now work with are increasingly different from you in terms of their tastes, habits, pop culture interests, and experience. Finally, that teacher preparation work you so eagerly undertook—and in which you most likely excelled—may seem murkier and hazier as the teaching days stretch on and as you swap stories and advice with teaching colleagues. Sure, you can depend on the experience you've earned in your years of teaching, and your teacher persona is probably quite well honed. But accomplished veteran teachers know that the job of learning is never finished, and they know that trying to teach English well is a challenging, even humbling, struggle.

WHAT HAPPENED?

What happened to you and that assured, confident person you were when you entered your first classroom?

What happened—and is still happening—is the journey of being and becoming a teacher, a *continuing* journey that is compelling, even exhilarating, but also uncertain, fraught with difficulties, never finished. In this book, we talk with you about how you have changed, how your classroom and school have changed, and what you can do to take your teaching to the next level. Our focus in this first book of the Continuing the Journey series is texts—literary, informational, and literary nonfiction—and we hope to provide you with not only support but also solid activities and wide-ranging resources to help you continue your journey to becoming a better teacher. After all, since the first year you began teaching, those texts and the best options for approaching them have also evolved. As we change, so changes virtually everything about the world around us.

George Couros, whose *The Innovator's Mindset* has captivated many educators, says, "When I first started teaching, I remember thinking that students should learn the way I taught; they should adjust to me. I could not have been more wrong. A great teacher adjusts to the learner" (38).

And the need to adapt to students and the larger social and political contexts of teaching and learning is not simply some sort of artificial and external professional goal; adapting is essential if you wish to stay in the classroom as a functioning, healthy, and effective teacher. Growing in your teaching is a way forward, a way to stay fresh and engaged; staying the same is stagnation and also an invitation to become less positive, less enthusiastic, and less effective. This is not what you saw yourself becoming when you first entered the classroom. It is not what you want for yourself or what we want for ourselves, and it's not what we want for you.

That you are reading this book is a clear sign that you too are interested in staying fresh and engaged as a teacher. You may know, as we do, other teachers who are less energetic in their professional growth. Writing a book such as this is a bit of a balancing act, as we seek to honor the great work veteran teachers do while acknowledging that some veteran teachers seem somewhat defeated. All teachers—including us, of course—can always find room for improvement. While we raise issues and concerns that may not reflect you as a teacher, see if you can recognize the teacher you might have become if you had not kept your passion and nurtured your spark. And we would love it if any aspect of this book helps you to rekindle the kind of enthusiasm for professional growth that inspires colleagues who have lost their fire or have allowed it to dim.

CHANGES IN YOUR PERSONAL LIFE

So what are the changes you are confronting? First, you have changed as a person. Just by moving through the years, by getting older, you have a more complicated life than you did when you first started teaching. Whether you entered the classroom right after college, came later to teaching as a career change, reentered teaching after some time either at home or in a different career, today you likely have more obligations, more responsibilities, more possessions, and more societal and familial expectations than you did years before. All of these can be immensely satisfying, a big part of your identity as a human being, but they all also complicate your life. The time you need to prepare for class, grade papers, and participate in other school-based activities is competing with the time you need for significant others, children, parents, extended family, and community. The mental energy you need as a teacher is divided between your professional obligations and the many hats you wear as a functioning adult. People write frequently about work-life balance—and this concern affects both men and women—but there are few convincing stories of how anyone, all the time, can balance the demands of a profession, a family, a home, a community, and a life. This is especially true of teachers.

As a teacher with a sincere commitment to your students and to your profession, this tug-of-war on your time is most likely a constant source of friction and, for some, discouragement. It's probably not what you imagined your teaching life would be, and if you have not been able to resolve some of these tensions between a complex personal life and a demanding professional life, it means that you are a teacher who is under almost constant stress. It can feel as though you are under siege. And you are not alone.

A recent article in *The Atlantic* reports, "Forty-six percent of U.S. teachers say they experience a lot of daily stress—that's more than what the nation's doctors report, and the topmost among other professional categories, level with nurses" (Walker). The article also explores aspects of what puts teachers under stress, and there are—no surprise—numerous culprits. The article maintains, "For many American educators, the current teaching arrangement appears somewhat grim: Schools expect a lot out of their teachers, without providing them with sufficient training and time during the school day to carry out their many roles and responsibilities" (Walker). Similarly, a Learning Policy Institute report (Sutcher et al.) notes that "contrary to common belief, retirements generally constitute less than one-third of those who leave teaching in a given year. Of those who leave teaching voluntarily, most teachers list some type of dissatisfaction as very important or extremely important in their decision to leave the profession." And once they leave, few come back: the report observes that "only a third of teachers who exit the profession ever return" (Sutcher et al.).

CHANGES IN YOUR PROFESSIONAL LIFE

Despite the daily stimulation of teaching and despite the wonderful students who come into your classroom every day with high expectations to be challenged—and sometimes also entertained—it is quite possible that you, at some point in a school year, are just overwhelmed. You may find yourself dealing with symptoms of anxiety and depression. A common shorthand term for this is *burnout,* and it affects many in the classroom (Chartook and Weiner; Draper). And, truth be told, burnout affects many outside of education, where, in our busyness culture, long hours, deferred vacations, and being constantly available, in touch, and online are almost perverse hallmarks of success and pride. It can be exhausting (see in particular Pang's *Rest: Why You Get More Done When You Work Less,* which makes an argument about the power of rest—for all of us). In the last several years, political pressure and constant changes in curriculum and testing have pushed many veteran teachers to new levels of stress.

Ken has experienced this firsthand:

THERE WAS A PERIOD *a few years ago when preservice teachers in New York State were suddenly required to take all new certification exams, including a time-consuming and overly technical portfolio called edTPA. High scores were set for these assessments and very little time was given to preparing teacher education programs to get their students ready for the changes. At the same time, new legislation was being prepared to allow commercial operations to begin producing teachers. It was difficult not to see these changes as motivated entirely by corporate greed and arranged to make traditional teacher education programs fail, opening the market to profiteers. The first semester these changes took place, I watched a group of highly intelligent, motivated, gifted graduate students crack under the pressure, one by one breaking down into crying fits as they tried to jump through a set of flaming hoops that did nothing but distract them from learning about real learning and real teaching.*

I had to stay resolute and confident for these preservice teachers and my colleagues at Stony Brook University, but in private I was a mess. I became consumed with the absolute certainty that our students would fail, that our program would be shut down, and that twenty-five years of service to English education would come crashing down around me. I had trouble sleeping, I couldn't focus effectively on work, and work-life balance was a joke. Getting through the days was a serious challenge, and the job I adored had become a source of almost crippling anxiety. With the love of an understanding spouse and the calm guidance of a professional therapist, I was able to get slowly back on track and then to start fighting back, getting involved in the teachers union and other advocacy efforts. The images of my adult students convulsing with sobs from exhaustion and fear—which still upsets me enormously—also fueled these efforts, helping me find the strength to speak truth to power when I had opportunities to confront those who made the dubious decisions that threatened all I hold dear.

I was lucky that my negative experience turned around; but I will never forget the hopelessness and depression I experienced in the depths of this struggle, and my heart goes out to the many educators (particularly K–12 teachers) dealing with it now.

The sense of hopelessness and depression related to burnout is a real phenomenon, not just a soft excuse for those who can't keep up. In education the statistics are stark and remarkably consistent over recent decades. As an initial point, who actually stays in teaching—who makes the first cut and continues on—is a surprisingly small group, because about one-third to one-half of *all* beginning teachers leave the profession in the first five years (Ingersoll). For those who stay, and you are one of them—congratulations!—the challenge continues and, in some cases, intensifies. A 2013 Metropolitan Life Insurance Company survey revealed that only 39 percent of US teachers said they were satisfied in their careers (Rankin 3), and a 2015 American Federation of Teachers survey of almost 30,000 teachers noted that while 89 percent had been very positive about teaching at the beginning of their careers, at the point of the survey only 15 percent were similarly positive (Rankin 3). This may also be true of you.

Many teachers are overwhelmed. They are committed and talented. Yet they are ready to quit. What has changed?

CHANGES IN YOUR CLASSROOM AND YOUR SCHOOL

If you feel that your professional life is less satisfying, beyond the conflict between your personal and teaching lives, another reason may be that your classroom and school district, your school landscape as it were, have changed. Like Ken's challenge regarding the imposition of edTPA, a foundational shift may have occurred in your school context. Your school and school system are, like most in this country, under tremendous pressure to show student achievement and student learning, and like most school systems, the one ubiquitous way chosen to "conclusively" demonstrate success is through student test scores. Reading and language arts are prime territory for routine, large-scale testing, and you and your students are undeniably affected. Even if you don't have students in your everyday classes who are required to take end-of-year high-stakes tests, you and your students are part of the testing landscape in your school system, and all of you are affected.

Additionally, if you are like many teachers, your students' test scores are used as a routine measure of your own effectiveness as a teacher, a requirement for states to earn federal funds during the Race to the Top era. Responsible school administrators at all levels are fully aware that good teaching is only one component of what leads to successful test scores, and that test scores are only one potential sign of effective teaching, yet it is routine to look at student scores in direct relation to those students' teachers. The factors you cannot control—if for some reason your students' home lives are now in transition or difficult, if they are undergoing or have undergone recent personal upset or even trauma—are not accounted for in large-scale test scores. Likewise, if you have students for whom English is a new language or students who are living with a disability, their test scores may be assessed and reported without consideration of those factors. And all of the successes you have helped students to achieve that aren't measured by tests may be ignored, or they may only show up on standardized tests years later. And yet today, teachers and school administrators live and die by these narrow numbers, and politicians and the press often use them as clubs to beat educators with whenever it suits their interests. Education can be a grim game.

Add to this national concentration on test scores the routine changes any school district will make every few years. Grade reporting systems change; requirements regarding lesson plans are altered; report format and frequency are revamped. New technology that your school may wish to implement can mean a serious shift from, for example:

- Paper notebooks to laptops
- Chalkboards to interactive whiteboards

- Overheads to document cameras
- Pen or pencil to Google Classroom, Blackboard, Moodle, or some other electronic platform
- Print textbooks to ebooks
- Oral class discussion to Twitter chats, or to an inclusion of back-channel discussion
- Uses of the latest electronic platforms and apps for everything from record-keeping to communicating with students and parents outside the school day

Student and teacher participation in social media, once prohibited, may now be encouraged as an asset to school learning. Smartphones, once shunned, are now viewed in some schools as valuable educational enhancements, and teachers are urged to incorporate them in lessons, in addition to other student-owned technology. The textbook series you may have been comfortable with is now replaced with electronic links to pieces of literature, websites, and clips from YouTube; organized by Lexile score; differentiated or translated with a click; and tracked by parents and administrators. The Harlem Renaissance poems you routinely taught in grade 10 are now replaced with a career- and college-readiness curriculum. Because students and their needs change each year, teaching has always meant aiming at a moving target, but now it feels as though the target's rocketing around like fireworks and we're shooting muskets.

If your school is conscientious, these changes will be forecast well in advance; you will have training in the requirements, both software and hardware; and you will be offered follow-up professional development that will reinforce the skills needed for new procedures and materials. In practice, however, few schools can quickly effect this kind of extensive training, and another stressor for you as a teacher is the need to hurry up, catch up, and do the new thing very well *right now*.

In addition, the move across industry for employers to stop providing training and instead to require that employees keep up on their own has migrated into teaching. Our profession is not immune to these changes in industry standards. In Ken's home state of

New York, for example, recent legislation has shifted the requirement for school systems to offer or approve teachers' continuing education credits to state-approved (outside) providers. It's now entirely up to individual teachers to find, achieve, and keep the records for the 100 hours of professional development they must accomplish every five years to keep their professional certification active. This is a new ball game.

CHANGES IN STUDENTS

Students also change. While verities of human nature endure, you have seen shifts in demographics in your school system and shifts in general student behaviors. Some of these are well documented and nationwide; some are more local. In Leila's home state of Virginia, there is a nearby school system that at one time was mostly rural and consisted of small farms, towns, and some suburban developments, all white and all middle class. It is now home to a large percentage of agricultural workers, people of color and second language speakers, whose low wages and seasonal work result in the stressors of working poverty and also in intermittent homelessness. For all the positives—students come to school with more than one language and with rich life backgrounds—there are some negatives, mostly related to economics. Food insecurity is now an issue in this county's schools as it never was before, and some students are routinely sent home during the weekend with backpacks filled with food. Ken knows of districts in his home of Long Island, New York, where young students are asked to take home "extra food" because it supposedly won't fit in the school's storage area; it's the only way some families can eat.

Along with these challenges come great advantages. A more ethnically and socioeconomically diverse student body allows students to bring a larger range of experience and perspective to classrooms. Multilingual students enrich school discourse and exemplify the ability to think through different worldviews. So much more interesting literature is available from authors from different nations, cultures, and socioeconomic levels, all of which can inspire engaged class discussion among diverse students. In short, many schools now more closely resemble the dynamic, ever-shifting culture(s) that exists beyond the school walls.

The point is that teachers must adapt to all of these changes—positive and negative—as their students change. And even when these changes are inspiring and richly satisfying, the adaptation they require from teachers can be a source of some anxiety and even pressure.

There are also external pressures on teachers and school leaders. In a local school system in Leila's area, a decade of continued state sanctions for low test scores and lack of accreditation continues to churn changes in the schools' curriculum delivery and achievement reporting; the atmosphere of system-wide school failure is a stressor for many of the teachers and administrators, and the continuous turnover in staff and superintendents exacerbates the problem. For these educators, the consistent cycle of new plans and programs, once greeted with hope and enthusiasm, is now a source of concern, fatigue, stress, and even hopelessness.

In Ken's community of Long Island, with a population close to eight million, schools make headlines, some for achieving national academic recognition and others (as little as a few miles away) for violent gang warfare. Leila's Richmond, Virginia, area is not as much in the headlines, but many students and their families routinely experience gun violence, home invasions, and community disruption. From helicopter parents to drive-by shootings, the constant pressures teachers face take a toll as they focus on helping their students learn as much as they can in order to face a future full of uncertain promise and possibility.

Students are truly the only reason we English teachers do what we do. On the other hand, all of the changes in them, positive and challenging, create some level of stress on us as teachers. Teaching is a labor of love, but it is very much a labor. Perhaps only other teachers can truly understand that.

THE TEACHERS' LOUNGE WE ALL WISH WE HAD

None of us can stop, change, or transform the landscape of American education and society. Certainly many of the forces that affect our classrooms on a daily basis are large ones, economic and demographic, and far beyond the scope of individuals, even when they band together as a group to speak with one voice. So, not surprisingly, nothing you read in this book will make these stressors go away or immediately transform your personal or professional life. Don't we wish we had that power! But there are ideas and strategies—and the companionship and wisdom of other teachers (such as Sonia Nieto's terrific 2003 *What Keeps Teachers Going?*)—to guide all of us. There is, indeed, help and direction to be found.

Imagine an ideal Teachers' Lounge, where along with the tables and refrigerator, the coffeemaker and the cups, we have a space where we are supported and safe, where we can talk about the changes in ourselves and in our school landscape that are not only concerning at times but that are also affecting our students and our sense of ourselves in the classroom. In that Teachers' Lounge are wisdom and insight as well as specifics about planning, grading, presenting, and selecting.

We would like this book to be, in a small way, something like what you would find in that ideal Teachers' Lounge. We, Ken and Leila, talk often to each other about our challenges and successes, and we find the conversations immensely rewarding and energizing. As you read further, you'll see that we've included in our ideal Teachers' Lounge many other voices from classroom teachers we admire and well-known English educators whose NCTE presentations are standing-room only. We think of the ideal Teachers' Lounge as a goal for this book because veteran teachers don't need step-by-step guidance or long explanations about best practices. They need quick advice, understanding, encouragement, and signposts pointing to innovations they can use in their classes. And they need these from teachers who respect their knowledge, experience, and time. This is the kind of Teachers' Lounge we all sometimes wish we had.

Leila recalls such a time:

I DESPERATELY NEEDED *such a Teachers' Lounge in my third year of teaching, when I had moved from a small Catholic high school to a large and boisterous public school. For me, the transition was beyond rocky, and even though I was aware that my students and I were clashing, that I was uneasy in my own classroom each*

day, and that nothing seemed to help me get my footing, I hung on. One of the more maddening aspects of changing to this school was that the English department chair blithely insisted that everyone belong to the local English teachers' professional association, pay dues, and attend the occasional meeting. The first Saturday I found myself in the stark, overlit cafeteria of Cave Spring High School, seated with other veteran English teachers and asked to share, I was both irritated and scared. I had nothing positive to say, just a litany of failure and fear. So when my time came to speak, I sketched something fairly grim and waited for the ensuing criticism. And it did not come. The teachers in that group were well aware of what I had described, had dealt with something similar themselves, and also had some few mild suggestions. As Maya Angelou so famously remarked, "People will forget what you told them, but they will never forget how you made them feel," and this group made me feel relieved, better about myself, understood, and even hopeful. I continued to come to those meetings, utterly reaffirmed.

That is the kind of Teachers' Lounge we want for you. This is the kind of Teachers' Lounge we hope you will find in this book.

Imagine, for example, you've had a long day in the classroom. Not a bad day, just long. Everything went fine but was uninspiring. You wonder what it means to have taught for several years and to have so many more ahead of you. How do you face this? What new goals can you reach for? Who except a fellow or sister teacher understands the malaise that can build from the exhaustive repetition of the school day? Before you head home, you stop in the Teachers' Lounge for a cup of tea for the ride home. You crack open the door, and Penny Kittle is sitting there, waiting to chat with you. Penny Kittle, the highly respected author of *Book Love* and *Write Beside Them!* You ask your colleague, "Penny, how do I stay inspired as a teacher?"

FROM THE TEACHERS' LOUNGE

Earn the Title Every Day

Penny Kittle
Kennett High School, North Conway, New Hampshire

Teaching requires heroic persistence. Parker Palmer, author of The Courage to Teach, *says there is a tragic gap between what is and what we know could be. You will see that gap in your teaching and in your students. Being a better teacher means you build a bridge to reach every student, plank by plank, day by day.*

First, be in love with your content—and remember that love will dim without attention. Marinate in your content: be an insatiable learner. English teachers read, write, and create. History teachers feel the hum when they near the topic subject or time period they love most. Your content is a subject, but so is teaching itself. Teaching is not an act, but a subject of continual study. Keep reading, exploring, thinking, and questioning. Listen to your students and learn from them. Believe in better, not perfect.

This work is labor intensive and even more so, cognitively and academically rigorous. Your brain will be lit up all day and it will get tired. You need rest and music and good things to eat. Find people who love this work and cling to them, celebrate with them, and run to them for help. Look for opportunities to move our profession forward. And if you can't see them, create them.

Last, assumptions about students are dangerous. Kindness takes time, but every day you model how to live, and students are watching. Love begets love: the more you give, the more that comes. This is a life

> *lesson, of course, but teaching is life work. You are a role model, and that comes with the awesome responsibility to show up and earn that title every day.*
>
> *Be someone to believe in. Bridge the gap.*

An ideal Teachers' Lounge is a place where real support is offered. A high school teacher, in a recent NCTE Connected Community online discussion group, reached out to ask for help to address the extreme burnout she was dealing with. The description of her situation was pointed and compelling, and it generated much discussion within the online group at the time. We reprint here from the online discussion teacher Deborah Alvarez's six-point answer to her colleague. It is a heartfelt and gifted response, timely, positive, and wholly supportive. For us, teachers like Alvarez would be the center of our ideal Teachers' Lounge:

> I have been there. It is not a pleasant place to be. I have listed some things that I had to do when I was faced with this. I hope that it helps you to renew and replenish your teaching life:
>
> First, you have to remember that you have options. Those options may include moving to another school district, changing your job entirely. These are not the only options, but I want you to think that you are NOT stuck and consider your options. Go online and see what a professional job hunter might be able to do for you. Just look . . . see if anything strikes you. Sometimes, by entertaining that you have options, you discover what you may want to do to make a living.
>
> Second, extricate yourself from the drama at the school. Teach and engage with those aspects of the school day that give you joy, and then leave the school to engage in other things that are fun for you and your family. Take a yoga class, learn to make pottery. We have to break the cycle of stress/drama that often surrounds us at school. Then, do something that gives you some joy and comfort.
>
> Third, remember why you became a teacher. That passion and commitment are really stressed right now, and you need a break in order to find that

love again. It may not be easy to see this right now, so it will take time. You commented that you are working on board certification. So, I am assuming you love teaching the children; it's all the other "stuff" that is getting in your way. Too much drama! Eliminate what you can and don't participate in the drama.

Fourth, find other friends and people and fellow teachers . . . who provide you with laughter and a positive view. Being constantly reminded of the woes and drama every day by our fellow adults only exacerbates what we are feeling. You may have to change your behavior—adolescents bring enough drama every day. Find a good friend to talk to, and admit your feelings. . . .

Fifth, this will not change without your commitment to making the change. Nothing changes without doing something for yourself. Once you take control of this, you will be able to find a way to enrich yourself.

Sixth, what do you want for your work life? If you can define it, then you can find a position that will fulfill that. Once I began looking for an alternative to enrich myself and fill what I felt was an empty vessel, I had an improved attitude. The improved attitude will allow you to see things more clearly and make choices that are better for you. . . . This summer do something that is personally fulfilling . . . go camping, join a group, do something for yourself!!! You deserve this. It is so important to find a source of replenishment for your teaching soul and relief from the stress.

I hope this helps you to set you on a path to rejuvenate your spirit. You are not alone in this.

Good colleagues are often the best source of solace, understanding, and truly helpful advice. In an "*EJ* in Focus" article, Nancy Mack described nine ways to keep up your "Energy and Enthusiasm" as a teacher:

1. Identify What Makes You Happy in Your Classroom
2. Keep Learning from Your Students
3. Cherish Your Literacy [read and write what you love]

4. Find the Courage to Develop New Ideas
5. Find Joy in What Students Accomplish
6. Seek Things Other Than School That Give You Energy
7. Find Ways to Gather Positives [keep a journal, for example]
8. Claim Your Own Mentors
9. Decide to Think, Feel, and Act Differently [take control] (18–25)

Classroom teacher Mike Anderson provides in *The Well-Balanced Teacher* his list of four teacher nonnegotiables: teachers need to **belong** (feel positive connections both inside and outside of school); feel they are **significant** (and make a positive difference); be **engaged** (which generates energy and passion); and be **balanced** (creating routines and setting boundaries so they are not overwhelmed). These four strike us as helpful as we think of the strength—and the challenges—of being a veteran teacher.

And, while it may seem counterintuitive, there is also wisdom in reminding ourselves that, yes, we are teachers but we are also *more than* teachers. Veteran teacher Marie Gist writes of something she learned about her sense of self and the classroom:

> Let yourself off the hook.
> This is not an exercise in mediocrity, but an allowance.
> You deserve to breathe.
> You **need** to have a life.
>
> Bottom line: You deserve to be something other than a teacher. . . . Allowing yourself to have a life means that you are not shut off in your teacher hole. You exist outside of the school and interact with the "real world" you so frequently tell your students they will one day be a part of. A "real world" that, by the way, your students live in. We need to abandon this phrase altogether.
>
> I get my best ideas about teaching when I am being present in my life, not from scanning Pinterest or sifting through teacher blogs. These resources

> are great for developing lessons or retooling something you felt didn't land, but in order to be a force in the classroom you need to be present in your life. By reminding yourself of who you were before teaching, your authentic self will seep into the classroom. You don't need to be anyone other than who you are—a message we often tell our students, but frequently ignore ourselves. (Gist personal communication, 2017)

THEN AND NOW

We are not alone. And all of us have our stories. On the NCTE website, "Then and Now" was an idea Leila had as part of her work to celebrate NCTE's 100-year anniversary. She asked teachers to write a very short piece highlighting one aspect of their teaching—*I used to ____, but now I___* was the frame. She invited teachers to contrast who they were when they started teaching and who they are now. In the context of this opening conversation, three of those voices are especially pertinent to our Teachers' Lounge and how we become better teachers. The first voice is that of Sarah Brown Wessling, from Johnston High School in Johnston, Iowa, who wrote about her teaching:

> My passion for learning and teaching grows stronger with each passing day and experience. On the other hand, while passion may be a good place to start, it leaves the potential for a lot of gaps, so in the past nine years I've been filling them in, building bridges, and seeing the landscape of teaching and learning through a kaleidoscope rather than binoculars. In past years, I had to worry about the details. I'm not ashamed of that; the details were small and manageable places to begin, a foothold for the passion. But I worried about the kinds of details that can inhibit instead of inspire good teaching. I worried about the tardy passes, all the right forms, and the careful—nearly robotic—construction of a lesson.
>
> While there is still important work in the details, crevices that need to be packed, now the details are different. I notice the inconsistency of a student smile, the subtle shift in a reading habit, the nuanced voice in a piece of writing,

> and the way in which I can provide guidance and feedback to each student's learning process. I've learned to channel my passion so that it fuels enthusiasm and steady pursuit of learning goals. I now see the kaleidoscope of each learner—brilliant chips of color, constantly making patterns and creating pieces of art.

And, from Sarah L. Morris, Berkeley Springs High School in Berkeley Springs, West Virginia, her "Then and Now" directly related to herself as a student and young woman:

> I once thought being a teacher was being a superhero. Instead of a magic lasso, I'd have a textbook; I'd step out of library stacks transformed. My students would see the "teacher me." I maintained the charade my first years. My classes were behaved, organized, and silent. The information was most important, and my task was deliver, assess, and raise student achievement.
>
> Eventually, I realized my ideas about identity were related to my teenage years—because I was different, I was not able to express myself in ways that enabled learning. If I embodied the perfect teacher stereotype, my kids wouldn't see my learning struggles. But accepting the idea that there was one kind of good teacher required perpetuating the idea that there is one kind of good student, which I knew wasn't true. If I believed this I would be rejecting my teen self, still there, hiding behind the dress and heels.
>
> Development of identity parallels intellectual development, and if we are unsure of ourselves we cannot succeed fully. My eccentricity is inspiring, and students can learn to be who they are by accepting diversity in me. Now, the first time a student says, "Ms. Morris, you are sooo weird," I know the real learning can begin.

And finally, something we talk about more later, from classroom teacher Amy E. Harter [Casey] of Sheboygan Falls High School, Sheboygan Falls, Wisconsin, whose mantra, *the joy stays consistent*, is a call to action for all of us:

> I'll never forget the wave of certainty that washed over me in an urban classroom, packed wall to wall with eighth graders, on September 16, 2008. That was it. I

knew I was a teacher. From that first day of student teaching, I felt a joy that motivated me—the joy of hearing students read their writing in their own voices, of seeing them debate and uphold new ideas. I witnessed, with captivation, emerging power in my students to impact their communities and become incredible scholars.

Since then, I've learned thousands of things about effective practices, classroom management, curriculum design, and assessment. I've changed to respond to different schools, students, and initiatives. Looking to the future, I know my career will be an evolution. But even after all the changes, *the joy stays consistent.* That unchanging aspect of teaching is the thread holding the shifting world of my career together. [Emphasis added]

A DISCUSSION STARTER

Consider the list in Figure 1.1, compiled by some of Leila's preservice students regarding what they wish they had known before they began their lives in the classroom. How many of these are things you too wish you had known? How many are things you are still dealing with? Are some of these your stressors? Take five minutes to use this checklist to see what you find.

Twenty-Five Things I Wish I Had Known

CHECK ONE OF THE THREE AND RANK THE STRESSOR FROM 1 TO 10, 10 BEING THE HIGHEST

	WISH I HAD KNOWN	ALREADY KNEW	NEVER THOUGHT ABOUT IT	STRESSOR
More classroom management techniques				
How to deal with/or teach students with disabilities or English language learners				
How physically demanding it would be				
How many red pens I would need				
How challenging the students can be				

Who in the school I can confide in				
That you have to "sell" everything you teach				
How to keep up with students who are absent				
The need to give clear, concise directions				
How to deal with different abilities in the same class				
That I wouldn't be GREAT all the time and it wasn't expected of me				
That I would literally lose my social life and still enjoy my life!				
That I have to repeat everything 5–10 times				
That grading takes even longer than anticipated				
That I need to call parents frequently and be open to their suggestions				
That students have bigger problems than my class and that's reasonable				
That not everyone likes reading and writing				
That if a student sees the activity is relevant to them they don't ask, "Why are we learning this?"				
That students may not pay attention no matter what I do and that I will say directions in a dead quiet room and no one will hear				
How exhausting it is				
How to keep records				
How to write on a board				
How to be angry				
How to transition				
That reflection does help				

FIGURE 1.1. "Twenty-five Things I Wish I Had Known" list.

How did you do? Our hunch is that you checked more "Wish I had known" items than "Already knew" or "Never thought about it" items. We also suspect that there are a number of items in the 5 and above range as stressors. These are areas of concern and, again, this book addresses them. Even with great preparation, motivation, and determination, being an ongoing and successful teacher asks a lot of all of us, year after year.

Consider using the results of this survey to search for blogs or books on the issues raised or to begin conversations with trusted colleagues or even trusted friends who aren't teachers. Feeling a general sense of anxiety or malaise or burnout can feel too big to change, but breaking such feelings down into their individual elements can help us understand and begin to ameliorate them. Veteran teachers are resilient, and one way they exhibit that resilience is by checking in with themselves and identifying and acknowledging their own needs.

MENTORING

Many veteran teachers have revitalized their teaching and have felt renewed by mentoring new colleagues in their own schools, from local colleges (as student teachers), or through regional or national mentoring networks. Anna J. Small Roseboro, a National Board Certified Teacher, has taught high school in five different states and is now co-chair (with Claudia Marschall) of the Conference on English Education (CEE) Commission to Support Early Career English Language Arts Teachers (search the NCTE website for more information). This relatively new group is one you may wish to become involved in, especially if you are interested in mentoring new teachers. Anna is in the Teachers' Lounge now, where she explains why you might want to add mentoring to your professional life.

FROM THE TEACHERS' LOUNGE

Why Mentor?

Anna J. Small Roseboro
Calvin College, Emerita

What better way to ensure the quality and success of our new colleagues than to mentor, for example, through the CEE Commission

to Support Early Career ELA Teachers?! Being a veteran teacher or even retiring need not be the end of your growth as a teacher. Most of us know that teaching English is both the most important and the toughest profession, since success in every profession depends on some knowledge and skills in reading and writing, speaking and listening. We veteran teachers know our content, yes, but we have also developed insight and skills to adapt what we know in ways that inspire our students to learn. And we've learned to balance our personal and professional lives.

If knowledge, skill, and balance were the only concerns, teaching would not be nearly so challenging. Learning to navigate the shoals of administration, school cultures, and changing political winds is perhaps even more crucial to the success of early career educators. Adjustments, adjustments, adjustments. A new teacher's inability to adjust quickly causes the endemic dropout within those first five years in the profession.

Veteran educators can stem the flight of passionate, intelligent newcomers by offering ears to listen, and time to share stories. We can offer factual evidence from our years of experience—and our shoulders to cry on and arms to hug. We can cheer on our new teachers, coach them from the sidelines, and celebrate their achievements, as they surely will come.

Throughout this text, you'll learn different ways to approach teaching and you'll hear many other teachers offering support and advice. If you enjoy the conversations we've begun, you can use them to begin new conversations with trusted colleagues. Mentoring new teachers or organizing a group of veterans to discuss new ideas is a great way to take your own teaching to the next level.

CONCLUSION

Veteran teachers are the backbone of a school, and students stand on their shoulders. As teachers, teacher educators, and administrators, we know that the teacher-student relationship is what school is all about. Veteran teachers are the most likely agents of change for students and schools and the most practical first responders to changes in students and schools. This book honors the responsibility, the power, and the knowledge that veteran teachers bring to their work. Veteran teachers are not hostages to change; they accept, resist, harness, and adapt to change in all the ways that benefit students.

Teaching is a continuing journey, and during your time in the classroom your control can ebb and flow. You yourself have changed; your life has become more complex. In addition, your own classroom, school, and school district perpetually alter with new initiatives, ideas, and materials for which you are not always well prepared or occasionally about which you are not especially enthusiastic. But the work remains, as does your place in your classroom and your identity as a teacher. What will strengthen you on a daily basis? Feed you as you work with your students? In the area of teaching literary texts, what will help you become a better teacher? We turn to this in the next chapter.

Finally, we note the chapter-opening epigraph. The lines are from an iconic American poem but also part of the philosophy of the Hindu holy text the *Bhagavad Gita*. In his *Four Quartets*, T. S. Eliot refers consistently to Hindu philosophy, and the point is simply that we should pay much less attention to the results of what we do and the perfection of what he calls "faring well" than simply to the act of continuing on, "faring forward." This is not meant as a retreat from standards or excellence but a simple acknowledgment that the act of doing can, in and of itself, have its own reward and positive outcome. Our interpretation is that by *faring forward,* the *faring well* comes of its own accord. And when we are in the midst of a bustling, hectic day, with students coming in and out of our classrooms, the bells ringing, the announcements crackling over the loudspeaker, the laptops open, and the backpacks put away, faring forward may be the best life we can imagine.

CHAPTER 2

Making It New: What It Means to Be a Better Teacher

Students are alive, and the purpose of education is to stimulate and guide their self-development. . . . [T]eachers also should be alive with living thoughts.

—Alfred North Whitehead, *The Aims of Education*

Courage is more exhilarating than fear and in the long run it is easier.

—Eleanor Roosevelt, *You Learn by Living*

How do you make it new in your classroom? How do you become a better teacher? There are so many voices and ideas and exhortations, so many acronyms about behavior, so many teaching tips about "being the best you can be" that at times it can feel as though, for the umpteenth time, we are being offered a succession of gimmicks. But what we want to emphasize in this book is that becoming a better teacher is neither magic nor just working longer and harder; it's *seeing yourself differently and acting accordingly*. In the epigraphs above, famed educational theorist Alfred North Whitehead reminds us that teachers, too, have intellects and ideas, and he urges us to use them in the classroom. And the inimitable Eleanor

Roosevelt points out that while fear is indeed part of change, courage is ultimately easier. Both of these insights guide what we talk about in this chapter.

"Being the best you can be" is a familiar phrase, and when it comes to teaching, it is an absolutely worthy goal. While it may not seem enough to those who are not in the classroom, from our perspective, our daily teaching is rarely a home run, a touchdown, a perfect 10, a triumph every class period, and those who insist it should be are unrealistic and out of touch with the practicalities of the classroom. (Would that we could require all those who voice such nonsense to spend a month teaching in a real classroom!) Being great every day is out of reach for most of us, but being the best we can be and committing every day to being better are both achievable.

In teaching literary texts, the focus of this book, being a better teacher is something you can do and start on right now, today. And the general guidelines we are suggesting come from our own experience as literature teachers—of literary, nonfiction, and informational texts—and are also reinforced by recent observations of a wide range of veteran teachers.

Both of us regularly see student teachers, and we work with our former students who are now veterans in the classroom. But a year ago Leila decided to do a bit more and spent significant time traveling across her state to observe a variety of instructional settings.

FOR SEVEN MONTHS *I visited twenty schools in six school districts in Virginia, observing ninety-five teachers and ninety-seven classrooms. Schools included eighteen public schools, a juvenile detention center, and an independent (private) school, and the courses were English language arts at both middle and high school levels. English classes grades 6 through 12, honors, collaborative, remedial, and also Advanced Placement (AP) and International Baccalaureate (IB) were all part of the observations. Most of the teachers observed had at least five years in the classroom, and many were at the fifteen-year-plus level of experience.*

What I saw was, simply put, fascinating. Not every minute of every class was fabulous, but most were solid, and some were stellar, filled with excitement, interest, and real student engagement. I saw teachers juggle multipart assignments with small groups and differentiate instruction with long-term projects. I saw classrooms involved in graphic novels, classic plays, articles from Newseum, activities on Google Classroom and readwritethink.org, and Web searches for research papers. From these veteran teachers, regardless of their general level of organization or competence, I noted areas that consistently stood out and were key to better teaching and, certainly, more satisfaction from the teachers' perspectives.

So what advice would we offer you, a veteran teacher, as you think of making it new, becoming better in your teaching? What would we chat about over coffee (or stronger) in our ideal Teachers' Lounge? Here are five principal moves we explore in this chapter:

- Rethink your role
- Intensify student engagement
- Complicate the level of your materials and differentiate accordingly
- Resist total coverage
- Remember the joy

Making it new is not about learning new pedagogy or uncovering new content as much as it is about reflecting on your work and recognizing yourself as a credentialed and experienced professional. This level of professionalism comes with a responsibility to make decisions that always put your students' learning first. Doing so may require shifts in your thinking, variations in how you spend your time, even recalibrations of your behavior.

RETHINK YOUR ROLE

This is a big one. One of the things Leila saw in her recent observations was that most veteran teachers worked very hard with their students and in their classes. But in these classes, it was not always clear that students were working as hard.

What if we consciously try to flip the script, flip our classrooms so that the teacher is less the consistent talker/worker/director? Yes, this may be easier said than done, but much deep teacher fatigue comes from an unshakeable belief that everything depends on you, that you are the sole engine of your classroom. Sometimes teachers do all the work because they haven't planned something more interactive, but in many cases we find it's because teachers have instilled in themselves the idea that classroom progress rests entirely on their shoulders. They buy into the made-for-TV stereotype of teacher as savior. This hero-teacher identity is a recipe for intellectual, physical, and emotional exhaustion. (And it only works on TV.)

Instead, a veteran teacher should see the classroom as a space of shared investments. An old saying suggests that "school is where children go to watch adults work." That's the script we need to flip. At the end of the day, our students should be at least as tired as we are, or even more so—after all, they're young. They'll bounce back quicker!

So how do we rethink our role as a teacher and move from *our* control to *shared* control? The key may be in our own behaviors and beliefs about what an active teacher looks like. Think about it:

- Do you believe that you must earn every penny of your paycheck by always talking and directing in class? (We recall a colleague who had planned a cooperative learning class for a formal observation, and the administrator said, "Oh, you're doing groups. I'll come back when you're teaching.")
- Do you sometimes find yourself doing the thinking for your students, in discussions and small groups or even individual interactions, summarizing for them and interpreting for them?

- Do you feel pressure to answer most of your own questions? Give students such detailed directions and rubrics that their responses are virtually fill-in-the-blank?
- Are you able to stand back in class discussion, resisting the urge to repeat and extend student answers so that students listen more to you than to one another?
- Do you think every student need and every student question must be met or answered right then and there?

If these behaviors seem familiar to you and if you can see yourself changing at least some of them, it's likely that you can rethink your role as a teacher. It's also likely that your students will become hungrier for and more present in their own learning, not content to be spoon-fed.

Think about it logically. Think about it from your students' perspective:

- Why should I listen carefully in class when I know the teacher will repeat everything?
- Why should I puzzle out any kind of issue when I know that, if I wait long enough, I will be told the answer or answers?

Many of our students are savvy and efficient; it is we who consistently set up situations in which we are literally doing all the intellectual work and encouraging them just to listen and absorb. Our motivation for this situation is almost always laudable, but if we rethink our role as teachers, we can turn a passive classroom—where we are doing all the thinking, connecting, talking, and working—into something more student-centered and student-alive.

If we rethink our teacher role, we become catalysts, not servants or talking heads. Yes, we give up total, absolute control (or at least our fantasies of it), but we move the locus—and the agency—to where it belongs: our students. At first this can mean some silences in our classrooms and some puzzled student faces. If, however, we can move the responsibility from us to them, it's not only liberating, but it also means they will be learning far more than otherwise.

Of course, a classroom in which the students take control generally requires more work from teachers before class meets. Lesson and unit planning becomes far more important to ensure a set of goals and assignments in which the students take center stage. Consider this flipping of your classroom (a trendy term for the principle of preparing students before class) by assigning anything that students can do on their own (e.g., reading, watching videos, writing) and then using class time to have students work together on a project or discussion—ideally, something they genuinely enjoy—that requires them to have completed the prep work. So what do you do if (when) some students come unprepared to dive into the work? Ken has some advice about that.

IF SOME STUDENTS *don't come to my class prepared, I let them spend the period doing the homework while they watch the other students enjoy the (I hope) engaging, active, social assignment I've created for them. I don't chastise the students, and I certainly don't embarrass them. I simply ask that anyone who hasn't completed the reading assignment come up to my desk when the group work starts. I ask these students to sit along the side of the room to complete the reading. Then I let human nature take over. Usually students are disappointed that they aren't involved, and soon enough, they decide to come to class prepared rather than miss out. And if they don't, I speak with them outside class time about why they aren't engaging in the class. With secondary students, I involve their parents or guardians, escalating my concern if the behavior continues.*

Ken's advice is premised on the belief that nothing is preventing students from getting their homework done. Of course, that is not always true. If so, however, you must do some investigating and intervening. If a student is continually unprepared, find out if there's something else going on: the student is working to support his or her family; the student won't take books home for fear of bullying; the home atmosphere isn't conducive to getting work done. When something like this is the case, it's time to tap school resources to assist the student.

And it's possible that more than just a few students in your classes will not come prepared, which requires more from you than simply letting students complete the assignment in class. If this is a result of a negative school culture, that's a challenge that requires you to involve school leaders and counselors. If it's something relatively unique to your class, you might do well to explore new ideas for lessons and assignments to engage your students. One of the most powerful things you can do is to ask students directly about the situation—often our students can offer invaluable insight and can help us turn around difficult situations.

We're in luck! Just as we're ready for a snack and a good professional chat, we find Susan Houser in our Teachers' Lounge. A veteran English teacher retired from the Pinellas County Schools in Florida, Susan was named NCTE's Outstanding Middle Level Educator in 2011, and she served on NCTE's Presidential Team from 2014 to 2017. We're fortunate to find this busy colleague sitting down for a rare break. Susan knows a thing or two about what it means to be a better teacher, and she's willing to share some advice about the importance of keeping ourselves available to possibilities, no matter how busy we feel.

FROM THE TEACHERS' LOUNGE

Staying Open to Opportunities

Susan Houser
Thurgood Marshall Fundamental Middle School, Retired
St. Petersburg, Florida

As a veteran teacher of more than thirty years in education, my best advice to those of you still in the classroom is to take advantage of every—and I mean EVERY—opportunity put in front of you to learn. Never assume that you

already know everything after a few years under your belt. . . . One example I can point to was an opportunity given to me to teach to a remedial reading class—which I did not want to teach.

This particular group of eighth-grade students could conceivably bring up our AYP (adequate yearly progress); they were the only ones who could possibly improve enough in one year to make our scores go up on the infamous FCAT (a Jeb Bush–instituted and No Child Left Behind (NCLB)–inspired testing regime). My administrator's offered incentive was that she would allow me to do whatever I wanted, within reason, with this group of students. This was supposedly a READ 180 class, and many of you know what this kind of curriculum dictates—strict adherence to a canned curriculum and a method of presentation that doesn't allow for any deviation. I acted surprised that she would "allow" me to do what I wished in that class. I knew and had taught under that system with dropout prevention students and had walked away from it a few years earlier because of the restrictions the district had placed on teacher autonomy and instruction. Nevertheless, I decided to take her up on the offer and trust she would protect me from the district "coats" (observers who came into classrooms in groups of eight to ten and watched teachers teach).

When I walked into that classroom the first day, the students were not happy to be there; they'd had to give up an elective to take this class. But we set about the task of doing what we were supposed to do. After a few weeks of reading watered-down stories from the R-Book at students' supposed reading levels, the students began to revolt. They knew their peers were reading the real stories in their classes while they got the "baby" versions of actually great short stories and books.

We talked about how they felt about this: they felt degraded, as though they were being treated like dummies. They resented that implication, and we brainstormed about what we could do about the situation. The students decided we would get copies of the "real" literature, read it and understand it with my help, and do the same type of assessments and writing their peers were doing. They became excited and invigorated. They wanted to prove they could do the work that the other eighth graders were doing and would no longer accept the watered-down versions.

The results were phenomenal. The students became my favorite class, and they achieved amazing results on their high-stakes tests. We went on field trips to plays, I took them to the movies on Saturdays, and we built a reading community like none I had ever experienced before or have since with any group of students. I learned so much from these students about respect and how to raise the bar in my expectations. Every single time I moved that bar up, whether it was learning new vocabulary words or writing literary responses to what they had read, these students moved with me because we trusted each other and what we were doing. And I learned to trust an administrator who, prior to this class, I hadn't had a lot of faith in. She was, of course, looking to the end product of higher test scores, but she was willing to trust me as an experienced teacher to get the students there any way I could. She kept the suits out of my way and then dazzled them with our success. How could they argue?

My message here is not about how important the teacher is. It's not even that you must always avail yourself of the experiences and opportunities that come before you. It's that you have the wisdom to know which experiences will help you grow as an educator. Sometimes it takes a leap of faith, as this opportunity was for me. Sometimes it means taking a university course or a training that you loathe. Or reading a book with which you disagree. But wisdom can come as early as you allow it. You just have to possess the frame of mind to put yourself in a position to learn. When you learn, your students learn. I challenge every teacher who reads this to learn along with your students. It will be a point of wisdom later on for you. I guarantee it.

Teacher morale has suffered considerably in the last decade, as No Child Left Behind and Race to the Top policies, privatization narratives, and education reform public relations campaigns have taken direct aim at educators. Despite our attempts, many of us have internalized the ill-informed, unfair, or downright false descriptions of our work that have been repeated ad nauseam in the popular press. In some ways, what we are asking is that you take the negative voice that may be in your teacher head that consistently says, "I'm not good enough" or "I need to work harder" and change it to something positive and powerful: "I am enough." "I can manage this." This shift can help you cultivate an enhanced sense of your own worthiness (Brown), a sense that may be eluding you as you try to meet every need of every student every day (Brené Brown's TED Talk may be some of the best twenty minutes of your time ever spent). What if you came to school each day knowing, *really knowing*, that regardless of the challenges, you and your teaching are indeed *enough*?

INTENSIFY STUDENT ENGAGEMENT

If we as teachers can rethink our role in the classroom, one of the things that logically happens is an intensification of student activity and engagement. No, we do not want to cede total control to our students, but if everything depends on us in every situation, students become passive and distanced. This is a concern for veteran teachers because we get better and better at controlling a classroom, and we can become very good at being benevolent dictators. But when students believe it's our classroom, not theirs, it's easier for them to check out mentally and emotionally. Student engagement is a goal we all share, but often unintentionally many teachers block it or mute it at almost every step.

Consider:

- How about starting your classes with something more motivating than what Leila occasionally heard, on the level of "Open your Chromebooks" or "We will be working on Standard 10.8 today"? Can you forecast at the beginning of your class what will happen in the next forty to ninety minutes that will make students feel motivated, engaged, and not as though they're facing drudgery? Students generally participate more robustly if they understand the value of what they're doing, especially if they believe it has value beyond school, as much of our ELA curriculum does. Try being more creative in your *anticipatory sets*, creating a context that prepares your students for the thinking required for the lesson and that ensures they understand the value the day's lesson holds for them.

- What do you think of beginning a class with a choice of entry points: for example, one that requires sketching, one that requires discussion, another that requires written response to a question? Or an opening that allows students a choice among writing notes silently, talking with a partner, or reading a short passage?
- Can you give your students more responsibility in class, even at the level of routine engagement (e.g., handing out papers, distributing materials, writing on the board, finding the passage, reading aloud)? Anything a student can do to make the class run will engage that student and allow you more time to focus on higher-level teaching tasks.
- What would be the result of using specific, targeted student answers as a centerpiece for discussion? Can you begin to quote your students' comments and observations to one another without simply repeating them, so that their ideas are made more important and valued, their ideas become the focus of the discussion, become even the foundation of future discussions and writing assignments?
- What would happen if you build in student choice in even routine classroom events ("We can do A or B"; "We can extend this or end it now") so that students know they have more classroom control and agency? Choice has been shown to be an extraordinarily powerful factor in student motivation.
- Can you increase the number of student comments that go by in a class discussion before you intervene? Try testing yourself; see if you can beat your own high score.
- How helpful would be the use of surveys, in-class polls, and other methods to engage all students' judgments at once? Try asking students to use their hands to vote: "What do you think of Brutus's decision to leave the forum before Marc

Antony speaks? Hold up one finger for *it's an excellent idea*, hold up five fingers for *it's a terrible idea*." (Ken likes to add, with mock sternness: "If you hold up one finger, be careful *which finger* you use!") Then you can engage students in a conversation with one another about why they voted as they did. And you can all have some animated discussion when the students find out what goes down after Brutus leaves.

- Do you suspect that when students are largely scripted and controlled, they will never struggle, learn, and become independent? That they may never learn to apply their knowledge in their own lives when a teacher isn't there requiring them and showing them how to do so?
- Does it occasionally strike you that when we set all the rules, all the expectations, all the parameters, student engagement withers?

When we move the emphasis to students, they must read, talk, puzzle. They must ask questions and then listen to one another. Students are doing the heavy lifting in the classroom. If we use their examples in the discussion and are present as a teacher ("This is interesting to me" was one of the most powerful teacher comments Leila heard during an animated and successful large-group discussion), students will respond. Students may indeed resist such a shift at the beginning—and that shift might need to be incremental for many classes—but when students feel some ownership, some control, excitement and interest are geometrically increased. Veteran teacher Marie Gist writes of her own planning and teaching:

> Try to think of your lessons as fluid. When you're in the classroom, embrace the chaos and be present. If you start a lesson and a student asks a better question than the one you had planned—go with it. Abandon your meticulously paved path and walk on gravel. You have done so much planning, thinking, and research on the ideas or concepts you are teaching [that] everything will be okay—the execution will be different and more meaningful than you had envisioned. Learning is taking place. This is the goal. (personal communication, 2017)

We love Marie Gist's idea of walking on gravel as a metaphor for being open to students' input on this journey toward learning. Walking on pavement is easier, but gravel will get you to far more interesting places.

Sometimes intensifying students' engagement also means intensifying our own engagement as teachers. Alex Corbitt—a veteran teacher in New York City, whose Twitter feed (@Alex_Corbitt) is so rich with great advice that he's got more than 32,000 followers—says that part of being a better teacher has meant letting students see his writing process.

FROM THE TEACHERS' LOUNGE

Sharing My Thinking as I Compose

Alex Corbitt

The Bronx School of Young Leaders, Bronx, New York

Providing my students with examples of strong writing is an essential part of my teaching practice. Modeling is particularly powerful when showing students how to compose gripping narratives and logical arguments.

A major development in my instruction has been to write in front of my students, creating models during the lesson rather than before the lesson. This allows me to illuminate the inherent messiness of the writing process. As a new teacher, I would write sample scenes and critiques before class. My students would analyze the prewritten pieces and infer our rubric criteria. I soon realized that prewritten examples failed to highlight strategies within my writing process. My students could identify the characteristics of strong writing but were met with frustration as they struggled to put theory into practice in their own writing.

I now write in front of my students, sharing my thinking as I compose. I've learned to become transparent with my decision making and authorial intent. I am honest when I'm stuck and intentional when I revise on the spot. My students provide me with ideas and feedback throughout my writing process. We become peers in the endeavor, and when it comes time to turnkey writing techniques into their own work, my students proceed with the confidence and resilience to succeed.

COMPLICATE THE LEVEL OF YOUR MATERIALS AND DIFFERENTIATE ACCORDINGLY

One of the few concerning things Leila saw in almost 100 English language arts classrooms she observed was the use of text materials that were below student ability and appeared to bore students and to inspire them to move quickly off-task. Especially with nonfiction, in some classes students were presented with text that was one-dimensional and uninspiring. When the response to those materials—mostly vocabulary exploration and structural analysis—was initiated, it became almost painful to watch students spend forty minutes or so working—and not working— on material that was demonstrably thin and low level. Some students, of course, attempted to look busy, especially when the teacher came by their groups to check on progress. It seemed clear, however, that many students were disengaged and restless because what they were asked to do was not challenging or even interesting.

What might be alternative approaches?

- What do you anticipate would be the effect of using texts just above student comfort level, which is the Vygotskian sweet spot for engaged learning? Getting students to stretch just beyond what they are capable of doing without help, the zone of proximal development, keeps them engaged and increases their learning.
- To what extent could you complicate simple texts so that students are engaged at a higher level and are no longer bored and off-task because the follow-up activities leave time on their hands? For example, you could pair simple texts with a short, more advanced text (even just a paragraph from a formal study, a theoretical text,

or a complex poem). Or you could ask students to make critical judgments about a text, offering suggestions to make it better apply to their lives and experiences.

- Can you, conversely, every now and then, differentiate your curriculum by using texts to which students can feel "superior" (such as children's literature)? You can then complicate the subsequent activity or have students do something with the material out of their comfort zone—such as a multipart video or art project for an authentic audience.

Complicating student learning can also go too far. Like many educators, we question advice regarding the use of primary texts that present serious obstacles to student understanding and comprehension. One such set of texts we have heard seriously advocated for classroom use is primary texts from our Founding Fathers and Mothers, such as Abigail Adams's letters to her husband. The letters have great value, no doubt, but students—as well as most adults—are often flummoxed by the eighteenth-century vocabulary, sentence structure, and even discourse tropes. These factors make reading the letters an almost herculean task, and the effort, for many students, outweighs the possible benefits. Beyond that kind of very difficult, even inaccessible text, however, we need to bring into our classroom materials that engage and, yes, challenge.

We believe there is a middle ground. Discussing even just a paragraph or two from a complicated but interesting text can stimulate students' thinking: bring in a complex poem about the anguishes of love; a few paragraphs from a scientific study on addiction; a short passage from a newly implemented state policy; an excerpt from a theoretical work on antiracism; a screenshot from a website listing resources for growing organic foods. Even if students walk away from the class not understanding every aspect of a text (and we address this below), they will have encountered something stimulating and real. And they will learn how to approach such challenging texts and gain something valuable from their efforts.

RESIST TOTAL COVERAGE

You may well have read the literature multiple times either to prepare for a class or because you have taught this text for many years. Understand that that kind of repeated familiarity with a text can lead you—falsely—to want to cover every aspect and make sure that every student understands all of its parts. This can be—and often is—deadening to students. Kelly Gallagher puts it aptly: "Want to extinguish an adolescent's curiosity? Cover as much material as possible" (10). If instead you can treat a text as if it's the first time you yourself have approached it, you will find that your students—and you—will explore the text together and be far happier.

To recall how this feels, find a text with which you are unfamiliar, prepare it *very briefly*, and then bring it into the classroom. You will be surprised at the energy you generate when this text is for you, as for your students, new and undiscovered territory. If you are really brave, you might select a poem that still puzzles you or a prose piece in which you have difficulty following the argument. This sounds ridiculously scary (Leila's stomach clenches when teaching Ralph Waldo Emerson's essays and most of Emily Dickinson's work), but the benefit is there. You will not be the expert on this text, but an explorer with your students. It's a different role, and it can have surprising benefits. Other things to think about:

- What would happen if you allow students to individually read half of a play or a third of a novel's chapters? For some teachers, it may be anathema (even heresy) to forgo reading an entire text, but why not read excerpts and fill in the missing plot lines to get to the richest writing more directly? Reading less may sometimes be just the right scaffold for getting students to read much more sophisticated texts.
- If you can contemplate not reading an entire text, could you let a jigsaw about a reading be enough of an assignment for a short piece of literature? (And that means truly enough.)
- How comfortable are you as a teacher letting some student confusion remain about what each character did or what the fourth point of the essay might be?
- Could you occasionally "drop in" a text for reading and not analyze it and not test it, just read it for its own sake? What message might this send to your students about reading and about the world of literary, nonfiction, and informational texts?

- Is there a time that you could challenge yourself by selecting a text with which you have no real familiarity, having the class read it, and together creating an activity for understanding? (Yes, this takes nerve, but you're a veteran teacher. If *you* haven't got nerve, who does?!)

It is so difficult to let go of our hard-won expertise regarding *Macbeth* or *Great Expectations* or *The Diary of Anne Frank*. Every bit of our education encouraged us to display our knowledge, and displaying knowledge feels really, really good. And it feels and often looks like work we should be paid for. But when we let this go, we are better teachers because then we treat our students as the readers we want them to become. And this means *all* our students, not just honors, AP, and IB students, those whom many teachers routinely treat as sophisticated readers. All of our students need and deserve literary sophistication, and when we extend this to every student, we as teachers also become more engaged.

REMEMBER THE JOY

One of the more consistent veteran teacher behaviors Leila saw in her observations involved the start of classes. In almost every instance, the beginning of the period was a lost opportunity. There is no doubt that the five "passing" minutes or so between classes is difficult not just for students but for teachers: it is important to get materials straight, talk to students who might linger after the last class, confer with a colleague who may come into your room, check your email or voice mail. But even with those undeniable pressures, teachers should not lose the opportunity to connect with students and to ever so briefly have some sort of personal engagement with them. Stand at your door, greet students by name as they come in, and when the bell rings, do not begin class with a directive ("Get out your notebooks") or silence. This is your and the students' class, your shared time, and students need to be greeted, and, yes, somewhat inspired. Don't be a teacher who begins a class with the pedestrian and the mundane, with nothing appealing or interesting. This is a wasted opportunity. Think about the following:

- To what extent are you open to starting the class with something that will provoke student voice and student ownership? If so, you could try one of these:

  - What's something you heard today on the bus or at lunch that struck you and with which you really agree—or with which you would argue?
  - If, today, right now, you could change one practical aspect of this school, what would it be?
  - If somehow your life was more like a Disney movie, and a friendly genie appeared and gave you three wishes, what would one be?

  There are many ideas floating around like this, and if you can ask students something that they connect to or immediately care about, you will get them thinking, talking, and sharing.

- How do you feel about talking about what you and the students will be doing during this period, telling them what might be interesting or challenging or even hard for them? This can move students toward understanding why what they will learn is valuable to them.
- Are you willing to open the classroom for an appropriately limited amount of time by asking students to share something? Some events are of deep interest to students, such as who won a crucial game, a local storm that took out power or caused destruction, a school honor, a national event. You can even ask students if anything they have done or could do in class could be related to the event. Could they write something about the game? Could they research the storm, read informational texts about why power goes out? If ELA is truly related to all aspects of life and living—and we know it is—can you allow your classroom activities to prove it?
- If you have your students write at the beginning of class, can you have one or two share, without preface or comment, what they wrote? You can call on students randomly, and allow a "pass" now and then if a student doesn't want to read that particular thing. You might be surprised at the level of insight some students show in their impromptu responses. And this also means that student voice is heard specifically at the opening of class. This is a concrete way to show everyone that your

students' thoughts and ideas are the most important elements of your classroom; in fact, as you know, students' thoughts and ideas are the central things school should be for and about.

When students enter a classroom, they are entering a special space and time. To remind them—and you—that this is a platform of activity and interest, you must be intentional and conscious of how you start your classroom. You have planned and thought about this forty to ninety minutes; what positive and important learning can you convey to your students? When students feel that the time will be productive and interesting, they respond with a certain enthusiasm.

MAKING IT NEW

Both of us have had the privilege of editing *English Journal*, NCTE's flagship periodical for secondary English teachers. Although our times in the editor role were some twenty years apart, both of us remember many of our focus issues fondly, and when Leila devoted an issue to veteran teachers, she wrote at the time:

> As a beginning teacher, like most novices, I was bothered tremendously by the very newness of everything. In my first years in the classroom, I was creating new lesson plans, new tests, new approaches. I was teaching novels and plays and poems for the first time and, occasionally, also *reading* them for the first time. I was completing year-end reports and other school-related tasks that I had never before confronted. Like so many beginners, I was more than occasionally exhausted by the newness, the strangeness, and I longed for the time when the plans and the material and the routine would be familiar, even routine.
>
> Now, some 20 years later in my teaching career, I know that the challenge of the veteran is how to make it new *again*, how to recapture that freshness, that excitement, even that edgy fear that is part of a beginner's life. At times I recall those days with real nostalgia and wish, once again, that I was doing some school-related task for the first time. . . .We are not the novices, the sprinters,

> but very much the veterans, the long distance runners, and what we do to keep our strength and our pace for the duration of the race is the focus of this issue. (Christenbury, "From the Editor" 11–12)

You may feel the same way: routine, while comforting, can also deaden. And while the research was originally done with preservice teachers, Tom McCann and colleagues' work regarding positive and negative aspects of teacher perceptions is worth recounting in the context of being a veteran teacher. He and his co-researchers found that teachers who were likely to stay in the profession and even thrive exhibited certain characteristics, including:

- A sense of duty toward their students
- Interest in improving their own skills and maturation as teachers
- A willingness to tackle difficult school issues through strategic plans, peer outreach, and opportunities for change and growth (35)

How many of these characteristics are familiar to you? How many do you share now? For McCann and his researchers, these teachers made it new, and it made the difference in their classrooms and in their view of themselves as effective teachers.

Another aspect of making it new is stretching yourself and trying new things and new ideas. Let's stop into our Teachers' Lounge again. This time veteran teacher Victoria Alessi is there. A teacher in the Smithtown schools in New York, Vicki is well known for bringing engaging innovations to her classroom. After teaching for many years, Vicki knows something about the effort it can take to be open to change.

FROM THE TEACHERS' LOUNGE

Embracing the New in a Period of Change

Victoria Alessi

Great Hollow Middle School, Smithtown, New York

The past few years have been a whirlwind of change in public education, particularly in the area of English language arts. We've been

asked to embrace, understand, and implement new standards, new theories, new titles, new curricula, new acronyms, new assessments, and new technologies. This constant influx of change has inspired me to continue developing my craft as a teacher and to continue challenging myself as a learner. Teachers are learners. We're never done learning; our learning just takes on different forms as we move through our careers and our lives.

Intrigued and inspired by a conference I'd recently attended about implementing literacy centers in the middle school English language arts classroom, I raced to replan my lessons for the next few days. As I created the literacy centers, I felt myself doubting their efficacy and doubting myself as a teacher. I'd never tried centers before; I assumed they were unique to the primary grades. I wasn't quite sure how they would work with seventh graders during a forty-minute time span: What if I run out of time? What if my kids get off topic? What if they all need me at once? How do I manage thirty students as they rotate through six centers? What if this is a huge disaster?

I am pleased to report that not only were the centers not a disaster, but they were a tremendous success. My students responded to all of the tasks appropriately, rose to the challenge of self-directed learning, and in their reflections requested to "do centers again."

Sometimes change comes with growing pains, but it is important to remember that change takes time, and when we allow ourselves to be open to new opportunities, we can change our expectations, we can change ourselves, and we can change our students.

Something we would like to leave you with is the idea of sharing with your students. The best teachers we know have personal connections in the classroom, and they make those connections on a daily basis. As noted earlier, in a recent observation Leila heard a veteran teacher respond in a discussion with the important—and often not heard—remark, "This is interesting to me." With that one comment, the teacher and the students became allies in the classroom: they were thinkers learning together. The fact that a discussion could be mutually compelling—and that a teacher could share this with students—is powerful acknowledgment of the importance of our classroom and our teaching and learning. Simply put, even after all these years, it is a privilege to teach and to interact with your students in genuine thinking. Tell them so.

Ken experiences this newness especially when he brings new technology into his classroom. New communication platforms, such as Twitter, don't have established rules and haven't yet been well researched. And yet Twitter, particularly since the 2016 presidential election, has taken on tremendous influence in American life. When Ken talks about it with his students, he asks genuine questions about it, which he and his students tackle together. There are no established answers to which Ken is privy that his students are not. Those authentic, equitable discussions are pretty exciting for everyone in the class and are an example of how we can set up situations in which all of us, teachers and students, are on equal footing—and have somewhat equal expertise. Ken recently conducted a Twitter chat about Twitter with his class of first-year college students. Using the technology in this way, as well as talking about the technology was eye-opening for everyone. Yes, we are the teachers, but our students also bring rich resources into the classroom, and when we can create situations where they, too, are experts who share, their engagement flourishes. They have a stake in the class.

CONCLUSION

In Chapter 1 we shared Amy E. Harter's "Then and Now" story, which noted that in her classroom, *the joy stays consistent*. While this might seem unrealistic, it is solid advice for all of us. The joy of dealing with our texts and our students often is the heart of why we choose to stay and why we thrive. It cannot come all the time or even be counted on to appear regularly, but if we are open to the moment in our classrooms, joy can be part of our continuing journey as veteran teachers.

Isn't this what we all want for our classrooms?

CHAPTER 3

Literary Texts: The Surprise, the Pleasure, the Joy

There is no Frigate like a Book
To take us Lands away
Nor any Coursers like a Page
Of prancing Poetry –
This Traverse may the poorest take
Without oppress of Toll –
How frugal is the Chariot
That bears the Human Soul –

—Emily Dickinson, 1286

The teaching of literature in schools is as much strategy as it is the intelligent reading of a text. More often than not, a "bad" student is one with a woeful lack of tactical skills. In a panic, unable to provide what the system demands of him, he mixes up learning and culture. Pushed aside by the school system, he soon sees himself as an untouchable in the world of reading. He concludes that books belong to the elite and chooses a life without them because, once, he could not discuss them when exam time came.

—Daniel Pennac, *Better Than Life*

When we first began teaching literary texts, both of us had hurdles to overcome. In Ken's case, writing was his first love, his go-to, but many literary texts assigned to him in school did not spark his interest, and he often opted out of assigned reading that was not in his educational comfort zone. In Leila's case, she was an avid reader, but her favorite literary texts were rarely the kinds of texts included in secondary curricula, and much of what she was asked to teach was similarly out of her comfort zone. So, for both of us in numerous instances, the literary texts we were teaching in our early years in the classroom were not really familiar—in some cases we had hazy memories of reading them during our own studies as English majors but, more than occasionally, these were literary texts with which we had only a nodding acquaintance. Therefore, preparation for a day's teaching could be daunting. We faced unfamiliar or distantly familiar literature, and we had the added pressure of not only intensively reading and understanding it (perhaps staying just a few chapters ahead of the students), but then going into class and, faking some confidence, actually teaching it. We bet that, as you read this, you are sympathizing with some of our concerns, that you, too, may have had similar situations in your teaching.

After some years of experience, however, this changed for both of us and, most likely, also changed for you. The pressure of working with unfamiliar literary texts eased. In general, as veteran teachers, we now know and have mastered a wide range of texts that are used in most English language arts curricula, and we are far more comfortable with them. The language, the characters and plot outlines, the thematic and literary significance, the connection to other texts, and the kinds of activities that can make them come alive for students are now in our wheelhouse. With experience, we are far freer to experiment and work with finer aspects of these and other literary texts.

But challenges remain, and if we want to move our teaching of literary texts to the next level, what are some of the issues? Let's look at what to teach and how to teach it.

SOURCES OF LITERARY TEXTS

Often the literary texts we teach in secondary English are guided by an agreed upon, mandated curriculum and provided in either hardbound textbooks or online sources. The sequence and even duration of lessons and lesson segments are also often regulated. In addition, despite tremendous advances in technology that provide access to multiple platforms and configurations, many school systems across the country retain a traditional, largely chronological orientation (but occasionally thematic and genre approaches) to literary texts that harkens back to how hardbound literature anthologies were organized. Thus, in your school, American literature may be covered in tenth grade, British literature is for juniors, and world literature is reserved for seniors. The Search for Self or The Question of Justice may guide part of the ninth graders' literature study. Regardless, most English classes rely on a heavy dose of the canonical classics (which usually involve mostly nineteenth- and early twentieth-century texts) in British, American, and world literature. While some of those texts may be familiar and comfortable for you, another complicating factor is the reality that many required literary texts remain out of reach for our students. Indeed, how a teacher deals with this reality is one of the great challenges of teaching required literary texts in school.

CLASSIC/CANONICAL TEXTS

Whatever classic or canonical texts you are using in your teaching, or whatever sequence you are following, as a conscientious and accomplished teacher, gone are the days when you can, especially with complex texts, slide over the details. The "tactical skills" Pennac references in the epigraph at the beginning of the chapter are essential—and we, as teachers, need to provide them.

As lively and bright as many preservice teachers are, they are often flummoxed by Shakespeare's sonnets, difficult passages from *The Scarlet Letter*, and whole sections of transcendentalist prose. For some of these students, their typical well-meaning—but ultimately unhelpful—approach is to provide the scantiest of introductions and then to ask their own students to "get in your groups and talk about it," apparently hoping that general student discussion will magically solve the difficult issues of context, vocabulary, allusion, and general understanding. As a teaching strategy for these kinds of mature and complex texts, that approach is, frankly, irresponsible. With such literary works, putting the onus entirely on the students and hoping for the best shirks much of the teacher's responsibility. What is needed is a teacher's direct support and guidance for the difficult but irreplaceable work of providing context and, after some vocabulary work, wading into such texts section by section, even line by line.

An inductive or discovery approach is absolutely defensible with much literature, and adept and even not so adept students can come to useful conclusions and insights with much of what they read. With many classic and canonical texts, however, the expertise, even intervention, of you as an expert reader is essential. Students deserve our efforts to scaffold for them—even if we ourselves must do a fair amount of research and preparation beforehand. In general, the inductive or discovery approach rarely works with difficult or classic texts, and if you wish to have your students really understand and work with these texts, you will need to do research for yourself and employ direct teaching with them.

For some more advice, let's make a quick stop in our Teachers' Lounge. There we find our colleague Jocelyn A. Chadwick, who has done extensive work with canonical texts, and who as president of NCTE is very aware of the needs of English teachers and the resources available to them. We sit down to chat and ask Jocelyn what we might need to know when we approach the classics and "reimagine" the canon.

FROM THE TEACHERS' LOUNGE

Blending the Arts and the Literary Canon

Jocelyn A. Chadwick
Harvard Graduate School of Education

Reimagining the canon as we experienced it as students and as we literary critics have interpreted it does not have to be cast overboard. The canon has never been and should not be static, predictable. It is essentially and necessarily protean—it lives and adjusts and moves with humanity, reflecting it back to itself.

As an example, while working with students on various projects for the last three years, I have found using art, music, video, and primary source documents—especially very old, now digitized ones (e.g., slave narratives, nineteenth-century newspapers and magazines by women, African Americans, and the white periodical press)—of inestimable value. I combined this approach during a recent presentation of The Scarlet Letter *to high school juniors from both urban and suburban districts with pieces by Tim Rollins, a middle school ELA teacher and founder of the Arts and Knowledge Workshop in the Bronx. Rollins requires his students (Kids of Survival [K.O.S.]), primarily Latino boys, to read and discuss a canonical work before painting their interpretations, reflections, and ideas about the fiction or nonfiction.*

The effect of my combined approach, drawing on multimedia and digitized sources of primary source documents and examples of Rollins's work as another means of expression, helped my students to revise and reconsider their interpretation of The Scarlet Letter. *Their ensuing critical thinking and inquiry, their reassessment of and willingness to reexperience this canonical piece by harnessing new learning tools, clearly illustrated the pedagogical efficacy of this blended instructional pathway. I use it to work with teachers around the country, exploring with them how they, too, can implement this approach. (See Chadwick and Grassie's* Teaching Literature in the Context of Literacy Instruction).

Just recently, I have embarked on an additional project, using this method with incarcerated teen boys as part of an early intervention program helping them to develop literacy skills before their release.

Beyond Jocelyn's good advice, what we suggest is attention to the following when reading complicated and complex texts with students.

CONTEXT

Context is the most difficult scaffolding we provide for students but also the most crucial; it's what students *must* understand or know before they are able to read the text. Not giving this information will make the reading of most canonical literary texts frustrating and even fruitless. You may know that proponents of the Common Core State Standards (CCSS) and similar standards actually discourage us from offering students any context at all for the literature they read. Michael W. Smith, Deborah Appleman, and Jeffrey D. Wilhelm believe this is a serious mistake, as do we. In their *Uncommon Core: Where the Authors of the Standards Go Wrong about Instruction—and How You Can Get It Right*, they suggest that prereading activities and contextual background are essential. Focusing too heavily on leading students through an analysis of literature without a context to work from encourages teacher-centered rather than student-centered classes (79). And let us be clear here: Context does not mean telling students what the piece is about, nor is it a time to tell students everything you know about the author or the history of the text. Rather, context is about preparing students for the language, setting, and tensions they will experience in the text. Done well, establishing context not only prepares students to understand the text, but also to do so with at least some enthusiasm.

VOCABULARY

Vocabulary is a separate subject in itself, but we take it up here only in the context of reading literature. Before you use a challenging text in class, prepare instruction for words that are both crucial and unfamiliar; more than six or so in a short section will doom the reading, so select a small number. Once in class, you can ask students about these words—do they know them? (and they may)—but once students have identified the words as unfamiliar, you might need to provide definitions and, as a class, discuss the definitions. It's also a good idea to have students work to figure out some vocabulary by the context of the sentences as they read, but not if doing so will disrupt their reading too much, and definitely not if it will suck the pleasure out of the drama of the text. (We often wonder how authors of the past would react to what we do with their works in schools.)

ALLUSION

As above: prepare to highlight phrases that are both crucial and unfamiliar; more than three or so in any section to be read will also probably doom the text. Again, you can ask students about these allusions, but once they have identified them, you will likely need to provide context (and that can be done in the context frame already discussed). It's a mistake to try to acquaint students with every nuance of a text. Sure, identify a paragraph here and there and go to town with close reading. But don't do it to so much of the text that the students lose interest. You know that great pieces of literature reveal more of themselves with each reading; we urge you not to pull everything out for students on their first pass.

REMEMBER THE JOY AND RESIST TOTAL COVERAGE

If deeply understanding the text is just too hard, it will not be enjoyable, and if it is a total chore, students will lose interest and enthusiasm, perhaps even begin to resist. If you can concentrate on a few elements everyone "gets" and even let much of the piece remain a puzzle, you have most likely done your job with canonical classic texts. Total understanding and total coverage will ruin the work for these beginning and advancing readers.

We need to remind ourselves: our classroom is not graduate school. Middle and secondary English classes introduce young readers to great literature to which we want them to return someday, not avoid in horror or wince at in retrospect. In addition, we suggest that you not use this terrific canonical work you have selected as primarily a vehicle to teach literary elements; let those elements emerge from an understanding of the text itself. Such an approach will not only honor the text, but it will also make the literary elements more contextual—and thus more memorable. Reading a text should be a dynamic experience from which meaning springs to life; focusing on literary elements is more like an autopsy. Reading is not a visit to a museum; it's a safari.

WORDSWORTH'S "NUNS FRET NOT"

Here's an example of this kind of approach using a sonnet by William Wordsworth. "Nuns Fret Not" (1807) is short but deceptively difficult, fourteen lines of meditation and argument on how rules and restrictions are actually not confining but liberating. It's an interesting idea—it goes against what almost all of us in modern life would hold, and it has strong appeal as contrarian, if not truly unique, thinking. It presents a very different point of view and could well appeal to an age group that is highly sensitized to adult-imposed boundaries.

How does Wordsworth craft his argument? The illustrative instances he uses are direct and multiple, but the more than 200 years between the poem's first appearance and today can defeat our twenty-first-century students, even as the piece, clever as it is, shows how one artist can comment on an idea and also use a format (the poet is also restricted within the sonnet template) to reinforce the point. Wordsworth writes:

Nuns Fret Not

Nuns fret not at their convent's narrow room;
And hermits are contented with their cells;
And students with their pensive citadels;
Maids at the wheel, the weaver at his loom,
Sit blithe and happy; bees that soar for bloom,
High as the highest Peak of Furness-fells,
Will murmur by the hour in foxglove bells:
In truth the prison, unto which we doom
Ourselves, no prison is: and hence for me,
In sundry moods, 'twas pastime to be bound
Within the Sonnet's scanty plot of ground;
Pleased if some Souls (for such there needs must be)
Who have felt the weight of too much liberty,
Should find brief solace there, as I have found.

If we pursue some of the considerations outlined above, we need to ask questions and provide those answers in our classroom.

Context. You can begin the brief study of this poem by asking students to consider how a rule or a restriction can be a positive, even liberating, thing. Students face boundaries every day and in every aspect of their lives. Asking them what kinds of rules they confront will open a discussion, as will the rather contrarian idea that those rules might actually make life easier. This is the context of "Nuns Fret Not," and although the poet ends with a much narrower point (like these rules, he finds the fourteen lines of a sonnet actually a lot of fun), the overall issue in the poem is weighty and worth considering. Certainly not every student will agree that "nuns fret not"—they may well believe that those nuns are just aching to make a break for it—but if given context, they will be able to discuss and consider the points.

Some students are familiar with the idea of a convent, a nun, a hermit, and a cell (at least in a monastery, not a jail—or a phone!). Others are not familiar; you need to assess students' familiarity and provide context and background. Once established, most students will easily understand the basic comparison between a nun's or hermit's cell (room) and the world, as well as the later comparison between the fourteen lines of a sonnet and the expanse of other literary forms. Regardless, if you choose to use this poem, some sort of contextual background is essential; left to their own devices, few students will get the point—and the pleasure—of "Nuns Fret Not."

Vocabulary. For most modern readers, the six examples the poem offers to buttress its point are almost overwhelmed by an unbridgeable unfamiliarity. Once students realize that the poet is offering numerous quick examples to make his point, they will have to deal with the vocabulary of *nuns, cells, hermits,* and *citadel.* Students who love and know flowers may well understand the references to *foxglove bells*, but the British *Peak of Furness-fells* will probably elude them. *Wheels* and *looms* are not used in modern life. The verb *fret* and the adjective *scanty* may need explanation. To what extent you carefully and precisely unpack these terms is part of your teacher choice and craft—we believe that glossing all of them isn't necessary and will make "Nuns Fret Not" a chore. It's your choice as to how in-depth you go—but make no mistake, this sonnet will not have any impact unless students have some grasp of the point and at least a few of the examples the poem provides. And that means some vocabulary work.

Allusion. Wordsworth, like most in his era, was heavily influenced by Christian theology, so the "prison" to which he refers is Christianity's belief that human life is a sad sojourn on a sinful earth that is to be redeemed by death and then rebirth in a glorious heaven. The prison also relates to Wordsworth's own philosophy, expressed fully in longer poems such as "Tintern Abbey" and, specifically, in "Intimations of Immortality." In the latter, Wordsworth develops his thesis that human beings come into the world connected to the cosmos and "trailing clouds of glory"; only subsequently, with maturity, are they imprisoned in a cruel reality. (Students might be interested in pursuing this through some reading on Jean-Jacques Rousseau, an eighteenth-century French philosopher who advanced a similarly positive view of young people as opposed to the corruption that comes with age.) Whether students need to go into this in-depth is questionable; if a class queries the lines ("In truth the prison, unto which we doom / Ourselves, no prison is"), it is possible to pursue the discussion. Otherwise, this single reference may well be unnecessary to discuss at all.

With some preparation and direct teaching, as well as serious restraint regarding coverage, canonical literature can be a joy to your students. A light touch may be all that is needed to pique their interest for more—and, yes, we do want to keep them reading, don't we?

As you think about structuring reading activities for your students, it's a good time for us to see who's hanging around our ideal Teachers' Lounge to give us some additional thoughts. This time we find Kelly Gallagher, veteran ELA teacher in Anaheim, California, and author of the popular *Readicide: How Schools Are Killing Reading and What You Can Do about It.* Always good for some valuable perspective, today Kelly offers us an important caution about structuring students' reading too much.

FROM THE TEACHERS' LOUNGE

Let Students Do the Thinking When They Read

Kelly Gallagher
Magnolia High School, Anaheim, California

I encourage teachers to abandon the "side-by-side" approach to teaching novels. The side-by-side approach goes something like this: The teacher assigns Chapter 1 of a novel and then meets the students the next day with a quiz. The teacher then assigns Chapter 2 of the novel and then meets students the following day with another quiz. And so on.

There are two problems with this approach. First, students are not stretched as readers. When the book is chopped up into many pieces, the book ceases being a book; it becomes an extended worksheet. Many of our students are "click-and-go" readers, so they need to be coaxed to read larger chunks of text without teacher interference. It is important that students develop the ability to track their thinking over time. My students, for example, read a novel in four weeks, meeting once a week to share their thinking. The days of spending eight weeks to read one novel are over.

The second problem with the side-by-side approach is that the teacher is the one who always determines the thinking that occurs. When students answer questions posed by the teacher, their thinking is defined by the teacher. Instead, students need to be taught how to do their own thinking as they read. Any teaching done should occur after students have generated and shared their own thinking. I still teach novels, but I teach them from behind the students. They think and share first, and then I follow.

So what is my advanced approach to teaching literary texts? Let's ditch traditional quizzes, worksheets, and packet work. Let's stretch readers by having them read long sections of a novel at a time. Let's encourage them to generate their own thinking. In short, let's teach them to read books like we read books.

MULTICULTURAL LITERARY TEXTS

The days of needing to justify the importance—if not the moral imperative—of reading and teaching diverse literature are fading, and as you look for new sources of multicultural texts, or mine old ones, your assurance and expertise will be greatly appreciated by your students. There is a depth and richness to texts from outside the Western canon that both open a world to some of your students and validate reality for others. Reading a diverse range of literature is enormously worth our time.

Veteran teachers, white and persons of color, do not require a definition of multicultural literature or a rationale for including works from authors of color and from a variety of cultural backgrounds. So instead of presenting such an overview, we jump right into some of the advanced topics that emerge when teachers approach literary texts from a wide range of authors.

SOURCES OF MULTICULTURAL LITERATURE

Sources for multicultural literature are manifold, and recently lauded books, such as Jacqueline Woodson's highly acclaimed *Brown Girl Dreaming* (recipient of the National Book Award, Coretta Scott King Award, and NAACP Image Award for Outstanding Literary Work, Youth/Teens, and a Newbery Honor Book), are great choices for your classroom. The work of James Baldwin is currently undergoing resurgence, and writers from South America and Central America are also appealing, as are Commonwealth nation writers from countries as varied as India, South Africa, those in the Caribbean, and others. While many of these works deal frankly with mature themes such as violence, racism, immigration, and poverty, they bring with them compelling stories and crafted language. Michelle Jewett offers this list of authors to explore: Sherman Alexie, Leslie Marmon Silko, Louise Erdrich, Joy Harjo, M. Scott Momaday, Jhumpa Lahiri, Maxine Hong Kingston, Siddhartha Mukherjee, Khaled Hosseini, Haruki Murakami, Julia Alvarez, Junot Díaz, Isabel Allende, Sandra Cisneros, Eduardo Galeano, Jorge Luis Borges, Gabriel García Márquez, James Baldwin, Toni Morrison, Alice Walker, W .E. B. DuBois, Frederick Douglass, Maya Angelou, Richard Wright, Zora Neale Hurston, Ralph Ellison, Nikki Giovanni (95). J. D. Vance's *Hillbilly Elegy: A Memoir of a Family and Culture in Crisis* is garnering widespread attention and may usher in new works about the multiplicity of white cultures and socioeconomic class in the United States, which may also be valuable additions to your classroom.

For excerpts to share with students, you might also consider reading the following selected literacy (auto)biographies from academics of color (and many apologies for this admittedly partial list):

- Keith Gilyard's *Voices of the Self: A Study of Language Competence* (1991)
- Victor Villanueva's *Bootstraps: From an American Academic of Color* (1993)
- Carmen Kynard's *Vernacular Insurrections: Race, Black Protest, and the New Century in Composition-Literacy Studies* (2013)
- David E. Kirkland's *A Search Past Silence: The Literacy of Young Black Men* (2013)
- R. Joseph Rodríguez's *Enacting Adolescent Literacies across Communities: Latino/a Scribes and Their Rites* (2017)

SENSITIVITY TO CULTURAL APPROPRIATION

One consideration of which you are most likely very aware is that your own background—gender, race, and class—can play an extraordinary role in the effectiveness of your instruction. Such issues may well become more apparent and fraught as a result of the neo-Nazi, white supremacist rally and the protests against it in Charlottesville, Virginia, in August 2017, which—at least nominally—were about the removal of a Confederate statue. What a text (such as a Confederate statue) means is greatly influenced by who is interpreting the text and what history that person brings (or ignores) in their interpretation. *Handle with care* could be a pertinent cautionary phrase here. New teachers are consumed with learning the ways of a classroom and may be somewhat forgiven for being less aware of or less attentive to these cultural aspects of text; veteran teachers like us, however, must account for these aspects of reading and literature.

The mantra of *handle with care* can, first, apply to the issue of cultural appropriation, when a text is presented by a teacher—without complication—as authentic to a gender, culture, or race and it is not.

A *Washington Post* article defines the issue, at least in today's terms:

> Originally a piece of academic terminology, "cultural appropriation" describes the adoption of elements of one culture—food, symbols, traditions, fashion—by members of another.
>
> Such crossover is inevitable when cultures rub up against each other, and the outcome is often benign or even positive: Think of the music of Jerry Lee Lewis, or New York pizza. Yet there are those incidents in which the Western world co-opts without acknowledging the source of its inspiration. It can be demeaning to the culture it's borrowing from, perpetuate negative stereotypes or disrespect the sacred: Think African American hairstyles touted as hip summer looks for white women when black children are punished for wearing the same styles to school, Native American ceremonial regalia worn as unearned costumes, or slang seen as low-class when used by minorities but funny and provocative when used by whites. (Emba, n.p., Internet links removed)

As examples, we might look at twentieth-century southern white novelist William Styron's reimagination of the nineteenth-century slave rebellion leader Nat Turner in *Confessions of Nat Turner.* This is an iconic example; Styron's autobiographical approach to Turner was greeted by many critics with anger and scorn upon its publication in 1967. On the same grounds, protesters recently asked that a white artist's depiction of the murdered African American Emmett Till be removed from exhibition at the Whitney Museum in New York.

On another front, members of the disability studies community have adopted a mantra that indicates the need to ensure that representations of disability include voices of people *with* disabilities: "nothing about us without us" (Charlton). Patricia A. Dunn (*Disabling Characters*) has recently written on ways in which more authentic voices in disability can enhance students' study and understanding of literary texts that include a character with a disability.

Managing authenticity can be challenging territory even for seasoned scholars. *The Journal of Political Philosophy* was recently criticized for devoting an entire issue to the Black Lives Matter movement without including a single contribution from a black academic (Jaschik). The outcry from African American scholars about what the journal called "an especially grave oversight" is understandable.

Certainly there are many examples of artists and writers who present themselves in their work as different genders, cultures, and races; it is part, of course, of the writer's craft. In some instances, however, it's not seen as imaginative art but rather as theft and misrepresentation. It will be your job to pick and choose so that a text doesn't function as blatant cultural appropriation; it will be part of your job to contextualize the piece and explain why you are selecting and discussing it. For canonical texts you are required to teach, bring up the terms of cultural appropriation with your students and debate them. After all, there is nothing more authentically American than debating issues of cultural assimilation and appropriation.

SENSITIVITY TO DEROGATORY TERMS AND LANGUAGE

A second issue is how you will deal with the possible use of derogatory and incendiary terms. The latter is an issue in widely used canonical texts such as *To Kill a Mockingbird*, *Adventures of Huckleberry Finn*, *Native Son*, and *The Merchant of Venice* (among others), as well as in more recent works such as Sapphire's *Push* and Toni Morrison's *Beloved*. In the past few years in this country there have been numerous parent and community challenges to such works in the English classroom. Anticipating these issues may well save you some misunderstandings and concerns; indeed, if you are uncomfortable teaching these works because of your own beliefs, not from a fear of controversy—even with contextual preparation for both yourself and your students—you are best advised to avoid them and choose less personally problematic substitutes.

Lest this appear cowardly, do know that majority teachers (that is, teachers who are not members of underrepresented groups) bear a special burden when teaching works in which minority characters are disrespected or vilified. Contextualizing the historical veracity, for example, of Huck's terminology regarding his friend and traveling companion Jim, or interpreting the Maycomb, Alabama, townspeople's racist references to Tom Robinson, just may not be something you wish to pursue. Or, despite all your excellent attempts to provide an interpretation, the text may end up reinscribing biased cultural assumptions and misinforming, alienating, even harming, members of the school community. It may also be something you yourself do not believe and do not wish to bring into your classroom.

Ken had some experience with these issues in a first-year college seminar he taught in the spring of 2017.

THE STUDENTS WERE *assigned fairly randomly, so my sixteen students included seven students of color, three of whom were fluent in Chinese (one of whom used Google Translate to follow our class in English) and four of whom were African American; students in majors from English to engineering; students who were athletes, musicians, or members of student government. We focused on issues of social justice and social media, and issues of race came up often. The students were bright, open, and friendly, and most were willing to speak up—all to our great good fortune. At an appropriate point, a white male student said in a tone that was both respectful and sincere, "How come African American people can say the n-word [he said 'n-word'], but not white people?" Having taught too many classes in which there is only one student of color, often African American, I have learned not to ask*

that student to speak to such issues. Accordingly, I said, "Is there anyone who would like to address that?" As I asked, I scanned the classroom with my eyes a foot above the students' heads so I wouldn't catch in particular anyone's gaze and make them feel obligated to respond. In this class, I was happy—and lucky—when one of the students, an African American woman, spoke, and a lively, respectful conversation ensued. It was too detailed to describe here, and it didn't come to any resolutions, but the class ultimately came to understand that who is speaking is part of a message, so who you are when you say something matters. During the discussion, I asked follow-up questions, and I contributed things I believed some were probably thinking but didn't want to share. I noted things like, "Well, I know there are some people who think . . ." and similar points. I don't hide my personal views as a teacher, but in this case they weren't really relevant. My task was to keep things respectful and keep our discussion relevant to the subject matter. At the end of that discussion, I asked, "Who learned something valuable from this discussion?" and every hand went up, including mine. I didn't ask, but I assumed that many of us learned from one particularly intelligent, critical African American woman in the class—who I'm convinced is going to be a powerhouse in whatever field she chooses (of course, I dangled the idea of "English teacher" in front of her a few times!)—and also from the other students of color who supported her contributions.

I tell this story not to highlight my teaching, but rather to illustrate the fact that if as teachers we can be open and prepared for possibly controversial and uncomfortable discussions when they arise, we can be ready to have a truly teachable moment in our class. In this case, the context was right. But there have been (and will be) other contexts in my classes in which such rich discussion won't be as possible.

There have been times when I've been unprepared for such discussions—or for the directions in which such discussions have veered. I have, frankly, ended up feeling insecure and have verged on criticizing students for expressing honest but controversial or ill-informed views. At times I've had to stop discussions and take time to do some research, explain, apologize, and begin again in future classes. There have also been times, to my chagrin, when I've just awkwardly ended a discussion and hoped the topic wouldn't come back up. As you know from your own experience and from what I'm describing here, discussions that include cultural identity and social power are inevitably challenging. Despite this fact, they are also crucially important—perhaps more important now than ever, given the rise of anti-immigrant fervor and white nationalism/supremacism. Veteran teachers need to be prepared to guide positive, respectful, and well-informed discussions.

English Journal coeditors Julie Gorlewski and David Gorlewski published an interesting and controversial series of articles about teaching *Adventures of Huckleberry Finn*. In the main article, Peter Smagorinsky describes an assignment he's used with preservice teachers in which he replaces the n-word with another extremely derogatory term for women (the c-word) in order to cultivate empathy from white teachers teaching African American students. Several black female authors respond in the same issue to Smagorinsky's suggestion and raise questions and provide advice about negotiating these turbulent waters as teachers make decisions about what and how to teach (Leigh Patel; Ebony Elizabeth Thomas; Jocelyn A. Chadwick). This series is a must-read for veteran English teachers, especially those interested in thinking more deeply about the awesome and uncomfortable power of literature to cause as well as possibly assuage harm.

In an unrelated but also remarkable *English Journal* column, pointedly entitled "Speaking Truth to Power: Whitesplaining the Canon," Michelle Jewett says that it is still far too common to see "ELA teachers who have failed to examine the racist language and limited portrayals of people of color in canonical texts" and that we should stop teaching ELA as if it were a course in "Euro-American studies." Doing so means we must "replace canonical works with books that humanize people of color" (95). This also, of course, means ELA teachers, especially the 82 percent of whom are white (Boser, qtd. in Jewett), must learn about the rich cultures and histories from which noncanonical works come.

It comes down to this: particularly as a veteran teacher—a duly-credentialed professional compensated by the community to provide effective, proper education—it is your responsibility to use your professional judgment in your selection of materials and to be responsible for the fallout. Being apolitical is simply not an option, as every decision an English teacher makes about what and how to teach has a political dimension. This is why we need a powerful and wide-reaching Teachers' Lounge, to think through such issues with our smart and experienced colleagues. If your professional judgment is usurped, remember that there are organizations to which you can turn for help; in particular, NCTE's Intellectual Freedom Center provides powerful support.

Multiplicity enriches all of us, and we embrace the privilege of being an American and being surrounded by difference and benefiting from all the good things that come from difference. Cultural learning is an honor and a fascination. We are stronger as a people—and as readers, writers, and thinkers—when we immerse ourselves in the complexity of multiple cultures.

This is another good time to take a break and step over to the Teachers' Lounge. R. Joseph Rodríguez is there just now, and he has some important words about how English teachers can enact the kind of pedagogy that empowers and preserves culture. Incidentally, you'll be hearing a lot more from Joseph, as he is incoming coeditor (with Toby Emert) of *English Journal*. He's also got a book coming out in 2018 titled *Teaching Culturally Sustaining and Inclusive Young Adult Literature: Critical Perspectives and Conversations*.

FROM THE TEACHERS' LOUNGE

Culturally Sustaining Literature

R. Joseph Rodríguez
California State University, Fresno

Others are fighting too, even in the Garden, where sometimes it feels like there's not a lot worth fighting for. People are realizing and shouting and marching and demanding. They're not forgetting. I think that's the most important part.

—Angie Thomas (443–44)

How does a teacher sustain literature experiences that are giving, vital, and whole in the lives of young people who are coming of age in our classrooms?

The reading and study of literature can provide moments of engagement, reflection, and remembrance in the literacy journeys of children and adolescents. We teachers can guide our students as they read literature from various cultural experiences and worlds and also enact literacies across the communities to which they belong. More specifically, literary selections and conversations that reflect our country's pluralism are essential for a democracy that includes chaos, struggle, and turmoil.

Culturally sustaining literature unfolds in and out of the classroom and in multiple ways through the elements of literacy, including you (readers/literati): knowing, listening, memorizing, noticing, observing, performing, questioning, reading, speaking, thinking (metacognition), viewing, and writing (wonderment) in our lives (Rodríguez).

Schools are sites for our students' growth and change, especially through literature that can sustain students' cultural knowledge and ways of being, knowing, and understanding themselves in the presence of the familiar, their classmates, and diverse communities. In fact, our students will meet literary characters who may change them, characters for whom they may develop empathy and with whom they form a bond, as well as characters they may be indifferent or resistant to, even characters who help them "become citizens of the world who can make ethical decisions" (Alsup 6).

Alim and Paris remind us, "Culturally sustaining pedagogy exists wherever education sustains the lifeways of communities who have been and continue to be damaged and erased through schooling" (1). In our teaching of literature and as readers and teachers, we can affirm and sustain our students' coming-of-age, cultural knowledge, and identity formation across the literary and informational texts we teach.

Care and sensitivity cannot always overcome the blunt realities of racial prejudice, suspicion, and a legacy of discrimination. Leila experienced a situation a number of years ago that helps to bring home how difficult and painful this can be.

I REMEMBER A STUDENT *who in a senior AP class I was teaching challenged my right to select and teach Richard Wright's* Native Son *(Christenbury, "Race Differences"). Miguel's heartfelt contention was that no white teacher—such as I—should use this novel in class and presume to discuss it either as a piece of literature or as a piece of social justice. This was an uncomfortable and ultimately unresolved conflict for me. While the novel stayed in the AP curriculum that semester, the objection by this African American student was honest, if unsettling, and neither the class time I devoted to discussing the issue of appropriation and cultural ownership nor my one-on-one discussions*

with Miguel ever resolved the conflict. Despite my attempts at reconciliation and attention to questions of appropriation and identity, Miguel never accepted my authority to teach Native Son*—or even my authority to critique his class responses to* Native Son*. He maintained for the entire school year that I, as a white teacher, had no standing to engage in any dialogue regarding such a text. And his deep feelings persisted: when I saw him and some classmates at a local restaurant the summer after their graduation, everyone else at the table greeted me and smiled. Miguel just looked away.*

You may never have such a situation in your own classroom, whatever your background or ethnicity, but do know that the issue is of great seriousness to many, and at some point you may need to consider it, make your choices accordingly, and deal with the consequences. These cultural (and power) issues challenge the best minds in our field, and they can and should challenge the best minds in our classrooms.

We have focused in this chapter on issues of race and ethnicity; however, there are certainly other sources of discrimination that should be taken up through literature, including ableist and heterosexist biases. To learn more about how issues of disability might be addressed in English, see the issue of *English Journal* guest edited by Patricia A. Dunn, titled "Re-Seeing (Dis)Ability," and her "Disabling Assumptions" columns in more recent *EJ* issues. For more information about raising LGBTQ issues in English, see "Sexual Identity and Gender Variance," an issue of *English Journal* guest edited by Paula Ressler and Becca Chase. For a more recent and very thorough investigation, see sj Miller's 2016 *Teaching, Affirming, and Recognizing Trans* and Gender Creative Youth: A Queer Literacy Framework.*

CONTEMPORARY LITERARY TEXTS

Bringing into your classroom up-to-the-minute literary texts can be extremely satisfying, and your students, if they become engaged, can be powerful source seekers of those texts.

While very contemporary literature can be controversial and even questioned if not first reviewed and sanctioned by your department, team, or school board, contemporary literature often has a power and immediacy for students that older texts do not.

Think of current magazines (such as *The New Yorker* and *The Atlantic*) or online zines (such as ShadeZine or Shabby Doll House) that feature short stories, poems, artwork, and more. For other sources, go online and check out websites such as NCTE's readwritethink .org and the American Library Association book lists at ala.org; find book titles through awards such as the Newbery, Michael L. Printz, Pura Belpré, Coretta Scott King. Reputable bestsellers are also great sources (see lists from the *New York Times, Washington Post, USA Today*). Goodreads and the librarian-created A Book and a Hug website can be sources, as well as the winners and short-listed finalists for the Man Booker Prize, National Book Award, and Pulitzer Prize, all solid sources for contemporary work that, with some investigation, you can bring into your classroom.

One recent example of a popular work you may want to read and use is Donna Tartt's Pulitzer Prize–winning *The Goldfinch*, the story of a young man who loses his mother in a tragic accident and faces a moral dilemma. While the novel features some violence, drug use, and strong language, the grief of the main character and the ethical issue he faces are compelling, and the prose is gorgeous. Issues of being young, motherless, and adrift may well speak to your students, and the alternating locales of Manhattan and Las Vegas provide some range of setting in this lauded novel.

Interest in dystopian literature is currently at a high mark, and Canadian Margaret Atwood's *The Handmaid's Tale* (again, some caution here as there is sex and violence galore) may appeal to your students, with its vision of a society in which, in the name of peace and order, human liberty is severely curtailed.

YA AND GRAPHIC LITERARY TEXTS

YA literature is undergoing a renaissance of sorts, and not only are the current books and book series garnening wide public and adult attention, but also the tie-ins with film are omnipresent. Harry Potter (in Rowling's series of the same name), Katniss Everdeen (Suzanne

Collins's Hunger Games series), Hannah Baker (Jay Asher's *Thirteen Reasons Why*), and just about any character in the novels of John Green (*Looking for Alaska, The Fault in Our Stars, An Abundance of Katherines, Paper Towns,* etc.) are enormously popular with middle-level and secondary students, and the reading of these books deserves your attention. Consult also the Assembly on Literature for Adolescents of NCTE (ALAN), which runs an active website (www.alan-ya.org), publishes a fascinating journal (*The ALAN Review*), and hosts an annual conference that attracts hundreds of young adult literature enthusiasts to dynamic meetings with popular authors and respected critics.

As noted earlier, dystopian literature is also undergoing a renaissance, and if you feel that Ray Bradbury's *Fahrenheit 451* and George Orwell's *Animal Farm* and *1984* are showing their age (and, yes, despite their classic stature, they are), any of the YA series Uglies, Hunger Games, or Divergent books may strike more of a chord with your students. *Z for Zachariah* (Robert C. O'Brien); *Feed* (M. T. Anderson); *The Last Book in the Universe* (Rodman Philbrick); *How I Live Now* (Meg Rosoff), and other such titles are also good dystopian choices. And while you read these newer works, it's a great idea to bring in excerpts from the older, canonical dystopian texts, to whet your students' appetites for them and to help them make critical connections.

Likewise, there has been an ongoing growth in graphic novels, and for the many students (and possibly their teachers) who define reading as something more than left-to-right decoding, graphic novels are great choices. Gene Luen Yang's *American Born Chinese* and Marjane Satrapi's *Persepolis* are both well-regarded accounts of young people in challenging circumstances, and they are complex and multileveled.

Another example is Australian writer Shaun Tan's *The Arrival*, a compelling and wordless novel that tackles immigration and all its rewards and stresses. Using a fantastical assortment of animals and humans, set against a mixed realistic and fantasy background, students can read *The Arrival* and respond with insight; as one recent reviewer notes, "the story resembles the adolescent experience of navigating high school for the first time, unfamiliar with the landscape, customs, and even the people who roam the dreaded hallways" (Solebello 82).

LITERARY TEXTS AND LINKS TO FILM AND WEBSITES

At this point in your teaching career you are probably confident enough to know that linking print literature to film and websites does not mean the death of your standards or, necessarily, that students will never read the original source. Use of film, websites, and even video games is actually a way to keep students engaged and motivated in your class. The key is comparison and treating the second art form as seriously as the first. If a film is shown only as entertainment (or, even worse, as a misguided reward), its relation to the text becomes totally tangential; if it is taken seriously, it can, on its own terms, be evaluated in relation to the text *and* as a film, website, or game. If a video game is based on a novel—how accurate is it? What kind of relation to the original does it have? And how does playing the game immerse the gamer in perspectives driven by challenges of the characters and settings of the novel? If a film melds two characters into one and significantly changes the ending, you and your students can legitimately discuss whether this makes for a better narrative. To what extent is the film faithful to the intent of the original text? In the context of this film, does that question even matter? These kinds of questions guide connections from text to other sources and make their use helpful and defensible.

A recent Netflix series based on Jay Asher's *Thirteen Reasons Why* could be a great starting point for students. The novel, centered on a teen's suicide, is well crafted. While the subject matter may be tough for some students and parents and has generated some controversy, exploring how an extensive, multipart series can be spun out of a relatively short book could provide real discussion material for class. What has been compressed, left out, expanded? How does the series enhance or diminish the original novel? What is the ethical dimension of presenting in class a work about a teen's suicide? It's also important to consider what informational texts a class could (or should) read as well in the context of novels about sensitive topics, such as bullying and suicide. We take up this aspect of teaching *Thirteen Reasons Why* in Chapter 5.

FROM THE CLASSROOM

How do accomplished veteran teachers handle literary texts and take them to the next level? The following are some brief vignettes from recently observed classrooms, snapshots that show good teachers at work with students, making literary texts come alive.

VIGNETTE: CONTEMPORARY LITERATURE

The focus this early winter Thursday is a rather challenging Margaret Atwood poem, "Sekhmet, the Lion-Headed Goddess of War," part of a senior IB English class. For the entire spring semester, the focus of the class has been poetry, in this case, four poets—D. H. Lawrence, Elizabeth Bishop, E. E. Cummings, and Atwood—and a generous ten poems by each.

It is first period, around 8:30 a.m. The English classroom is in a high school situated in a small city. Built in the 1960s, the school building shows wear, and the student demographics are lower middle to working class with a racial and ethnic heterogeneity. The white female teacher and her seventeen students, thirteen females and four males, approximately fourteen students of color and three white, are in a second-floor classroom that has high windows, bookcases, moveable desks, and a whiteboard.

Class begins. The teacher first reads the poem aloud and then asks students to read it on their open computers. As a third pass with the poem, students read aloud selected sections of "Sekhmet." Three readings of the poem provide a sense of familiarity and ease. The class now moves into a large-group discussion, a format with which these students are clearly adept and comfortable. In this case, however, the teacher makes a chart on the class whiteboard and provides headings of *Subject, Themes,* and *Devices*, and also asks students to consider (and also puts on the whiteboard) *Speaker, Audience*, and *Tone*.

For almost seventy minutes, this teacher and her students are focused on "Sekhmet," and the conversation is productive, wide ranging, and inclusive. Not every student participates—the males in particular are quiet in this class—but the teacher uses specific student comments to further the discussion, records student comments under headings on the whiteboard, and provides needed background on the poem as issues arise. The question of literary devices comes up, and students and teacher locate and discuss them within

"Sekhmet." As the discussion progresses, links to other Atwood poems are made. One student raises a question about the overarching "point" of the poem; following the student's lead, the class discussion turns to consideration of the issue.

More than an hour has passed since the beginning of class. The teacher then moves students into small-group work, the focus of which is defining a topic and analytic statement that will result in a writing assignment on "Sekhmet." Students open Google Docs on their computers, and until the final bell, students work and discuss.

In numerous, specific ways, what this teacher does is effective and exemplary. In a fast-moving yet well-paced class, she sets up situations in which students can consider ideas, discuss, and succeed. She:

- provides multiple "looks" at the focus poem so that students can hear and also read the text numerous times *before* discussion;
- has a method to record student comments in a coherent and visible way so that students' comments are not only clearly valued (by being reproduced on the whiteboard) but also serve as a visual record of the discussion to which the teacher and students can later refer;
- encourages students' answers (in this class, the teacher was heard saying multiple times, "Yes, go on"; "What were you going to say?," etc.) and builds on those answers;
- makes student answers the focus of the discussion (for example, near the end of class, when a student notes the "point" of the poem, response and exploration of her comment guides the conversation for some five minutes);
- links this piece of literature to others students have read in the poetry unit;
- moves class configurations, in this case, from individual, to large group, to small group;
- addresses the issue of literary devices only within the context of the discussion; and
- asks students to use their classroom discussion as a springboard to writing.

Overall, these seventeen students are almost all engaged for the duration of productive classroom time.

VIGNETTE: THE CANONICAL CLASSICS

In this class, the sixteen ninth graders are not as obviously engaged or academically focused as the IB students sketched above. It is a high school setting, and this veteran teacher has the challenging task of introducing the Prologue and act 1 of Shakespeare's *Romeo and Juliet*. The class is evenly divided between male and female students, and all are persons of color, as is the teacher. For almost two hours, with a twenty-minute lunch break in between, this teacher is focused and gets most of her students to focus. Her manner is engaging and indirect; she uses humor and some cajoling. She acknowledges in her interaction with students the difficulty of the text and, more to the point, she makes clear her quiet confidence that students will "get" *Romeo and Juliet*.

The teacher's planning and sequencing are deliberate; her persistence is steady and yet delivered in a light manner. There is never total silence in this class, nor are all students always engaged; two females, best friends, will not stop giggling and making faces to their friends in the class. They alternate their interest in each other with attention to the academic matter at hand. Two males, seated in the back, consistently keep their heads down on their desks, hoodies drawn up. One student, who has just ended a period of family homelessness, fidgets and keeps an eye on his backpack and the full liter Pepsi bottle he has placed near his feet. But, for the most part, this lively, talkative class is with this teacher and, indeed, with Shakespeare.

One central technique is the use of distinct and multiple introductory activities to get students to look at the language of *Romeo and Juliet* and also to consider the "point" of the play: a query that comes from a section in Google Classroom, "What do you know of Shakespeare?" the answers to which are projected for the entire class to see; a brief teacher-read biography of the Bard; a computer-mediated quiz on hip-hop language and Shakespearean language—which is it?—and students do not always choose correctly; an excerpted

TED Talk; an open-ended response regarding Juliet's parents and their control of Juliet's interaction with her "bae." Through these activities, most of the sixteen students participate consistently and, after ten minutes of interaction and response, demonstrate a general understanding of the play and of the language. Of course, some misconceptions remain—one student answer about Shakespeare's language and its difficulty is heartfelt but off the mark; she says that "this language is from the Dark Ages because no one knew how to read then."

Only after these multiple activities does the teacher move to a more directive approach, and for fifteen minutes she goes through the Prologue, line by line, first asking students to circle and underline connotative language and figurative language. She moves from the front of the classroom to the center, sits in a desk with students around her, and models the first two lines, reading aloud, pointing out connotation and figurative language, and then asking students to do the same and also note what the subsequent lines mean. The students then take over the remaining text and offer answers. Many answers are approximate; the teacher takes these answers as offered and moves on. At the end of the fifteen minutes, students have, to a remarkable extent, unpacked the fourteen lines and understand what the Prologue forecasts.

Then the easier part: the teacher asks for volunteers to read and assigns student roles. The level of interest is high; approximately a dozen students take parts and read act I aloud. They stumble over some language but continue on—in general, there is almost total silence as the lines are read. What has happened in the previous minutes has prepared this class to participate: scattered across the room, eyes on worn copies of the play, for the last thirty minutes before the bell these ninth graders hear and speak the language of *Romeo and Juliet*. The reading concludes, the teacher offers a brief summary and a writing assignment, and the bell rings.

What can't be wholly captured in this description is the tenacity of this teacher, especially when confronted with sixteen ninth graders who are chatty, then occasionally silent, and then mildly protesting about class procedures. Smiling, calm, persistent, this teacher spends her ninety minutes querying students repeatedly, moving into the text, never taking

No or *I don't know* for an answer. She relocates from the front of the class to the middle and continues to engage students through smiles, questions, and remarks. In sum, what this teacher does is exemplary. She:

- allows students to share what they already know of the author and work;
- links a difficult, canonical text to students' lives;
- addresses the language of the text and links it to contemporary and culturally relevant art (Shakespeare's vocabulary and language to hip-hop);
- works with students line by line to unpack the opening Prologue;
- has students take parts and read the play aloud;
- links the follow-up assignment to what has gone on before in class; and
- is gently persistent, engaged, and positive, leading students into understanding and even a mild enthusiasm.

This is highly engaged teaching, and it ultimately pays off because these sixteen students have, by the end of the class, a real idea of the context and plot of *Romeo and Juliet*.

CONCLUSION

As an accomplished veteran teacher, dealing with literary texts can often be the most comfortable and rewarding part of your teaching day. For students who struggle, however, as Pennac observes in the chapter epigraph, they need us as guides and assistants. Only then will the complex texts we are asked to teach become Emily Dickinson's "frigate," which takes the reader away from the world and provides food for our "human soul." If we can intensify student engagement through direct teaching, guidance, and carefully crafted classroom experiences, students can enter into the world of sophisticated and challenging literary texts. Once there, complicating the material and differentiating instruction is more possible. In the meantime, we must be sure not to smother the text with total coverage of every aspect and every part. We remember, as the best teachers do, that there is surprise, pleasure, and joy in literature, and we can provide in our classrooms a rich and supportive setting for that experience.

CHAPTER 4

Literary Nonfiction: Opening New Worlds

Truth is stranger than fiction, but it is because Fiction is obliged to stick to possibilities; Truth isn't.

—Mark Twain, *Following the Equator: A Journey around the World*

If it isn't true, it ought to be.

—William Faulkner (in response to a question, posed during a public lecture at the University of Virginia, regarding the "truth" of his novels)

Most of us were attracted to teaching for reasons that do not relate to mastery of skills or test scores—we became teachers for many other reasons and felt that in the classroom we might be the person to make a difference. So, daily concerns about skill mastery and testing notwithstanding, many accomplished English teachers believe that central to their work is the development of lifelong readers, students who will, after graduation, continue their reading—or even rediscover their reading—in their years beyond our classes. And literary nonfiction may be a potent key to developing and sustaining those lifelong readers. It is no magic pill, but literary nonfiction has advantages that novels, plays, and poetry often lack. What are those advantages?

ADVANTAGES OF LITERARY NONFICTION

First, the **range** of literary nonfiction may well appeal to our students: the genre includes highly personal accounts, such as memoir and the more traditional autobiography, as well as history, science, engineering, social relations, nature, humor, culture, art, music, sports, food—the list is virtually endless. Our students are curious about the world, and nonfiction may give them what they perceive are more credible and contemporary answers than those contained in the works of the traditional English classroom. We know as teachers that there is truth in Hansberry and Shakespeare, but our students may also search for answers in a world wider than the traditional literary canon.

Second, literary nonfiction has the advantage of being perhaps not absolutely true (more on that later) but certainly **fact-based.** Teasing out literary nonfiction's relation to fact is a topic for a longer discussion, but in general we can assert with some confidence that nonfiction is a strong reflection of the real. Certainly Faulkner's comment in the chapter epigraph is an acknowledgment of that fact. While we as teachers admire the art of creating and exploring imaginary worlds within fiction, poetry, and drama, a historical or realistic contemporary world often appeals strongly to many students.

Third, teaching literary nonfiction lends itself more readily than other literature to use of the part for the whole—the **excerpt:** it's challenging to take just one stanza of a poem or one act of a play or even a single chapter of a novel and present it in class as a coherent or even representative piece without having to spend a great deal of time on context; literary nonfiction, however, is more easily adaptable to consideration of selected, shorter pieces. For many students—and teachers—this is a real plus. Using well-considered excerpts can give students broad exposure to a variety of works, saving time, always a factor in our teaching, and helping to preserve student interest. Excerpts are also easily used to augment other texts and to add texture or depth to the theme of a text set.

Fourth, literary nonfiction is often quite **beautifully written**. It is usually deeply researched, and authors employ the full range of their language skills to bring their research to life. The most talented literary nonfiction authors hold equal fidelity to some level of truth and to the beauty and character of their storytelling. In many ways, this genre merges the best of truth and fiction.

For these four reasons (and you can probably think of others)—literary nonfiction's range, its characteristic of being fact-based, its adaptability to excerpting, and the high quality of the genre—literary nonfiction may take your teaching to the next level.

As an added point, the undeniable rise in interest and quantity of excellent literary nonfiction may make this corner of literature more adaptable and appealing to you and your students than you might otherwise have assumed. It may be just us, but it seems that the current state of literary nonfiction is enormously appealing. Many excellent works are being published every day that range from the seriously technical to the highly artistic. And this is good news for us as teachers: most English curricula require heavy doses of nonfiction and, as noted before, a number of our students are less than engaged with poetry, drama, and novels, hungering for what they call—rightly or wrongly—accounts of the "real world." Literary nonfiction can fill that void and can also be as aesthetically compelling as other forms of literature. We like the range of insight and activity that literary nonfiction inspires. Although many teachers have used works of literary nonfiction purely as mentor texts for student writing, we find that it also functions as something wonderful in itself. Be careful not to read it only in the service of skill work. Literary nonfiction is interesting in its own right and can keep our students engaged in their reading.

As you have moved through your own teaching career and life, it's possible that you, too, have become far more interested in and open to literary nonfiction. Much of Leila's reading world was ruled for decades by fiction, poetry and drama. When she needed to provide more choices for her students, however, she started reading nonfiction aggressively and became hooked. Ken, who originally majored in marine biology, was already an avid nonfiction reader before he found his true intellectual home in the English department. Whether our tastes have changed or the books have gotten better, both of us now read almost as much literary nonfiction as fiction, poetry, and drama. If this is true of you, you already get it. If it is not true of your current reading, you might want to delve more deeply into today's literary nonfiction. The time invested will pay dividends for you and your students.

SELECTING LITERARY NONFICTION

In the world of literary nonfiction, what should a teacher be aware of regarding selection? There is, of course, a current canon of literary nonfiction that is established and used in English classes across the nation. Anne Frank's *The Diary of Anne Frank* and Elie Wiesel's *Night* are probably the best known and most commonly taught, and the World War II–era stories of teenage Anne's life in hiding and the young Elie's experience in the extermination camps are compelling to students across the generations. Tim O'Brien's *The Things They Carried* is also an example (although O'Brien's work is not strictly factual but blends story as well), and his account of the Vietnam War from a soldier's perspective has the advantage of being stylized and exceptionally well written. *The House on Mango Street,* Sandra Cisneros's semi-autobiographical account of her childhood told in short, poignant vignettes, has become a staple in many curricula. Two other works widely used in English classes across the country are the classic graphic work *Maus* by Art Spiegelman about the Nazi persecution of Jews in World War II and English teacher Frank McCourt's *Angela's Ashes*, the award-winning memoir of his youth in Limerick, Ireland. Based on his own adolescence, Sherman Alexie's *The Absolutely True Diary of a Part-Time Indian* attracts more young readers every year, adding to the diversity of the canon. Sometimes called an autobiographical novel, Alexie's book is not strictly factual, but it's close enough that Alexie calls the main character in *Absolutely True Diary* his "literary avatar."

You probably know of other canonical works of literary nonfiction used in your school and school district, and a quick Internet search for "Best Literary Nonfiction" will give you access to more worthy titles than you could ever read on your own. In addition, reviews, bestseller lists, and award lists from sources you trust (the *New York Review of Books*, for example) can offer guidance. Following are some other sources for excellent literary nonfiction you may want to use with your students.

TRADE BOOKS

Beyond the established works cited above, some of the literary nonfiction you might want to offer your students will come from the world of trade books, works, like most of those already cited, written for adults and premised on a certain amount of informational background and life experience. For this reason, you will need to review trade books before using them or recommending them to your students. Often these works include frank discussions of mature topics. This is appropriate for adult readers but may require some selection or excerpting on your part for your students.

For instance, the wholly admirable *The Glass Castle,* Jeanette Walls's exceptional memoir of growing up with dysfunctional and yet highly talented parents, includes many scenes of parental neglect and childhood and teenage distress that are not appropriate for all students. Dave Cullen's exhaustive look at one of the nation's most shocking school shootings, *Columbine,* offers few easy answers and actually refutes what most consider the "story" of the teenage shooters and their deadly rampage. Anna Reid's *Leningrad*, a detailed and well-documented history of that beleaguered city during World War II, is similarly frank about the effects of the German blockade of Russian citizens, featuring, thanks to newly available contemporaneous accounts of the time, detailed accounts of starvation and brutality. Ron Chernow's well-known and meticulously researched biography *Alexander Hamilton* may fret some students who will learn about Hamilton's manic-depressive work patterns and his destructive romantic life, traits that may be inconsistent with an uncritical admiration of one of the nation's most influential Founding Fathers. The racial injustice and overt and covert violence detailed in three excellent works of American history—*The Warmth of Other Suns* (Isabel Wilkerson writing about the great migration of African Americans from the South to other parts of the United States); *Hidden Figures* (Margot Lee Shetterly detailing the African American women "computers" [as in those who *compute*] in the 1940s through the 1960s NASA program, now an award-winning popular film); and *The Immortal Life of Henrietta Lacks* (Rebecca Skloot recounting the story of an African American cancer patient whose resilient cancer cells revolutionized scientific research all over the globe long after her untimely death)—could be enlightening but also profoundly disturbing for some students. Part of the pathos of *Immortal Life* is the fact that the researchers at Johns Hopkins, where Lacks ultimately died, used her cells without permission from her family and with no subsequent compensation. Comedian Trevor Noah's *Born a Crime: Stories from a South African Childhood* is similarly serious, a harrowing and at times deeply sad and disturbing account, but one also filled with love, hope, and triumph. Noah's take on the value of language for creating kinship is especially appealing for English language arts teachers. And, while it's not particularly controversial, Neil DeGrasse Tyson's *Astrophysics for People in a Hurry* could bring out middle schoolers' geekiest tendencies: For instance, did you know we may have descended from Martians? That *dark matter* holds the universe together even though we can't see it or even detect it apart from the gravitational pull it exerts?

Bringing the world of nonfiction trade books into the classroom requires confident teachers who are willing to take some risks and to make some mistakes. As a veteran teacher, possibly with tenure, you have a responsibility to take these kinds of academic risks. But even as a tenured senior educator, you're not alone. Your English department or school district may well have created lists of literary nonfiction that will be appropriate for your setting and your students. For more guidance, you can use professional journal and newspaper reviews, as well as professional resources such as NCTE, the American Library Association, and great books such as those by Kylene Beers and Robert Probst and by Ralph Fletcher. You can also turn to one of the best-kept secrets in any school—your media specialist/librarian. "Your school librarian adapts and rebalances collections to meet changing curricular needs and is poised to collaborate on interdisciplinary projects," says Amy Jo Southworth, a veteran school librarian, in "Poised to Partner: The 21st-Century School Librarian" (95). This article is a treasure of ideas for collaboration.

Finally, consider that your class is not a monolith. In any class of students—especially in grades 6–12—a range of interests, experiences, maturity levels, and needs abounds. Use this range to your students' advantage by allowing them to select and read literary nonfiction and recommend it to you and to their peers. With guidance and organization from you, your class may become its own best literacy teacher.

Ken built an entire course around two nonfiction works several years ago.

I WAS GOING TO TEACH *a course in rhetorical analysis, but coming at that topic straight on excites only the nerdiest of rhetoric nerds (such as yours truly). So I featured two full-length works of literary nonfiction:* The Omnivore's Dilemma *by Michael Pollan and* The Happiness Project *by Gretchen Rubin. Neither book is about rhetoric, but both texts provided us occasions to use rhetorical theory to analyze claims and counterclaims and to examine other genres (such as research studies, infographics from corporate and government sources, and personal accounts). The absorbing writing of Pollan and Rubin allowed my students and me to be immersed in new topics together, and for me to use my academic expertise to help the students improve their analytical and communication skills. The course went well, and the students said they found the rhetorical theory relevant and useful. I can guarantee that would not have been the case had I not focused the course on those interesting literary nonfiction books.*

NONFICTION STANDOUTS: ORBIS PICTUS AWARD WINNERS

Another source for selection of quality literary nonfiction is the NCTE-sponsored Orbis Pictus Award, which honors "outstanding nonfiction" for young people and is a highly reliable guide. Orbis Pictus highlights the best nonfiction titles from the year and is a fine source of high-quality works as well as a reliable "filter" regarding the work's appropriateness and reading level. Award winners you might consider are the historical account of the early twentieth-century British explorer Sir Ernest Shackleton, whose ship and crew became caught in the ice of Antarctica and lived to tell the tale (Jennifer Armstrong's *Shipwreck at the Bottom of the World*), as well as anything by the meticulous researcher Susan Campbell Bartoletti (who regularly tackles sensitive subjects in books such as *Hitler Youth* and *They Call Themselves the KKK*). Just in the past few years, Orbis Pictus Award winners have addressed a wide range of topics from the invention of the Ferris wheel to explorations of locomotives, volcanoes, dinosaurs, astronauts, deep ocean creatures, Supreme Court Justice Ruth Bader Ginsburg, and writer E. B. White. The list of award winners is trustworthy and worth your time.

GRAPHIC WORKS

And don't forget the excellent graphic works that also address nonfiction topics. The three volumes of *March* (Book One, Two, and Three) are a fine exploration of the Civil Rights Movement and co-written by civil rights activist and US Congressman John Lewis (with Andrew Aydin and illustrated by Nate Powell). *Maus* and *American Born Chinese* have been previously noted; other recent graphic works of interest include an account of Hurricane Katrina and New Orleans in Don Brown's *Drowned City;* George O'Connor's *Journey into Mohawk Country*, translated from the Dutch and using primary documents; and the touching memoir *Fetch: How a Bad Dog Brought Me Home* by Nicole J. Georges.

NONFICTION ESSAYS IN PERIODICALS AND NEWSPAPERS

Finally, many contemporary essays constitute literary nonfiction, and excellent examples come from magazines and the opinion/commentary sections of major newspapers. As English teachers, we may immediately think of periodicals such as *Harper's, The New Yorker,* and *The Atlantic*, all of which include essays on a wide range of nonfiction topics, but there are also fine literary (not just informational) opinion essays in technical magazines about subjects as diverse as cars and car racing (*Octane, Car and Driver, Road & Track, Automobile*), the shipping industry (*Ships*), aviation (*Air & Space, Flight Journal*), hobbies (*Tropical Fish Hobbyist*, *Nuts and Volts*, *Parrot Magazine*), as well as perennial favorites such as the widely available *Sports Illustrated* and *Sports Illustrated Kids.* A quick Internet search of any topic plus the word *magazine* will result in interesting choices. Many English teachers shy away from these sources, but for many students, they open a world of literary nonfiction on topics that are immediately compelling to them. It is worth your time to check these out and to recommend them to your students. Don't forget to ask your students to look for trade magazines that interest them; you might be surprised and fascinated at what entices students once they learn what is available to them.

Leila has a story that may be pertinent here.

I WENT BACK TO TEACH *high school English after many years working at the university level, and after the experience, I did a whole lot of soul searching about what I had done and what I had failed to do with my twenty-two juniors in Trailer 11 (Christenbury,* Retracing the Journey*).*

One teaching segment during my time that did not go particularly well was a foray into literary nonfiction. I should have known better, but I wanted to capitalize on my own very new interest in the modern American West. Through a teaching friend from a western state, I had been introduced to a number of western writers and even met some of them. Terry Tempest Williams, Annie Proulx, Kim Barnes, and Judy Blunt write compellingly of life in Montana, Idaho, Wyoming, and Washington, and I was totally intrigued by their work. Bringing in a twenty-five-page chapter excerpt ("Salvage") from Blunt's memoir, Breaking Clean, *seemed ideal, and I gave to my students a brief introduction and the chapter to read.*

Blunt writes directly and dramatically about an eastern Montana blizzard that she experienced as a young girl on her family's ranch. For thirty-six hours the blizzard raged, and it featured 70-mile-per-hour winds and a wind chill of -116 degrees. Pastured outside and largely defenseless against this weather catastrophe, the Blunt family cattle herd was virtually wiped out. The details of the cold, the way the family tried to save their animals, and the hardships of working outdoors during that difficult weather event seemed to me to be compelling. Many cattle died during the storm and some lived maimed and damaged afterward, and the details of their sufferings are chronicled dramatically.

What's not to love? "Salvage" had drama, weather, death, gore, pathos, and heroism. My juniors, however, were polite but noncommittal. The two days we spent on "Salvage" went, but did not go well, and did not feature particularly lively class discussion or activity. For these suburban students from central Virginia, virtually nothing about "Salvage" rang true. Despite my love for this excerpt and my enthusiastic efforts to frame it, my preparation for the reading and discussion about the piece had not been adequate or effective; this nonfiction account was too exotic, too extreme, and far too distanced from my citified East Coast students' lives to have any sort of impact or even veracity.

At the end of "Salvage," Blunt writes that the Montana wind is telling us: "Watch your back . . . this land owes you nothing" *(60). Wise words—and when teachers like myself are blinded by their love of a text, students are not necessarily going to go along. My feeling is that, like the Montana land, our students owe us virtually nothing, and in this case my efforts to engage them in a text that was far too alien to their reality were too little, too late.*

USING LITERARY NONFICTION

Literary nonfiction is indeed literary and, as such, lends itself to a number of classroom activities with which we are all familiar: reading, discussing, and writing about literature. This is a good time to check in to our Teachers' Lounge to see what our colleagues recommend. As we pour ourselves a glass of iced tea, we see Doug Hesse, a highly respected writing teacher and coauthor with Becky Bradway of *Creating Nonfiction: A Guide and Anthology*. Doug's knowledge of literary nonfiction, in particular the nonfiction essay, is extensive. He encourages us to closely study with our students the moves writers make in creative nonfiction essays.

FROM THE TEACHERS' LOUNGE

Writing about True Things in an Artful Manner

Doug Hesse
University of Denver

Edward Hoaglund once wrote that the personal essay "exists on a line between what I think and what I am." George Orwell, in his famous essay "Why I Write," concluded "I could not do the work of writing a book, or even a long magazine article, if it were not also an aesthetic experience." In those two quotations (and a couple dozen more I could provide) lies one key strategy for teaching reading and writing literary nonfiction: analyze how the writer's story and experience enhance the work's ideas and, crucially and reflexively, analyze how ideas enhance our sense of the writer.

Literary nonfiction, after all, is writing about true things in an artful manner, a way that makes readers choose to read it, not just feel obliged. Primarily through strong narrative, an engaging authorial voice, and a style rendered visible through image, metaphor, and sentence rhythms, the prose of literary nonfiction is often meant to be translucent, not merely transparent. Something essential gets lost if the work is boiled down to a stark summary. Virginia Woolf noted that an essay should "lay us under a spell with its first word, and we should only wake, refreshed, with its last."

I recommend, then, that teachers of literary nonfiction choose relatively short personal essays that have strong narrative elements that are entwined with ideas or events "outside" the writer's direct experience. E. B. White, George Orwell, Joan Didion, Annie Dillard, David Foster Wallace, and myriad others will work. Have students sort passages in which (1) the writer is telling a story (or more than one) from passages in which (2) the writer is exploring an idea, reporting an event that happened to someone else, or trying to reflect on lived experience or connect it to something else. Once this basic division and shape is clear, ask a series of questions:

- *How else could the writer have arranged these elements?*
- *What's the particular effect of this arrangement?*
- *What passages were problematic?*
- *What's your sense of the writer?*
- *What kind of person is he or she?*
- *To what extent does your sense come from the "what" of the story the writer tells? From the "how"—that is, the way he or she tells it? From the writer's ideas, thoughts, or commentaries?*

Two examples, one classic and one contemporary, illustrate the possibilities. E. B. White's essay "On a Florida Key" narrates a languid, even boring vacation in a Florida cabin. White's nonchalant observation of an orange with "color added" leads him to write about a local movie theater where African Americans are restricted to sitting in a "colored only" balcony, and the piece is suddenly about racism and more. Rebecca Solnit's essay "Occupied Territory" begins with her walking a mountain trail above San Francisco Bay and encountering a threatening unleashed dog whose female owner refuses to call it back. She also narrates visiting a friend in prison. By the middle of the essay, however, Solnit is meditating on who has "freedom" in public spaces, about individual status, about the state of feminism, and about who is elected to office, before returning to another story about walking with dogs. Both White and Solnit intricately combine personal experience with larger ideas, one poetically braiding with the other.

With some direction and practice, your students can do the same.

CONSIDERING THE ISSUE OF TRUTH

The issue of veracity—how true is the truth presented—is central to the consideration of nonfiction. Mark Twain's comment in the chapter epigraph has much in it for us to consider. Certainly in this country, given the current political realm, we are in the midst of an ongoing debate about what constitutes undisputable fact, what is competing for veracity (witness the popularity of the new term *alternate fact*), what is interpretation colored by fact, what is interpretation independent of fact, or what is simply fantasy (in the literary world, a *fiction*; in politics, a *lie*). These questions need not be scary ones in your classroom (see our discussion of politics in the classroom in Chapter 6), and they can be springboards for useful, legitimate discussion and examination. Our colleagues in history and social studies deal with these questions all the time, and the entire field of revisionist history is largely based on the reinterpretation of previous conclusions, new archaeological finds, or shifts in a field's thinking. It is similarly important to do this in English class. In some ways, this is an extra benefit to bringing nonfiction into the classroom.

As students read literary nonfiction, they should, among other things, be asked to consider the basic trustworthiness or veracity of a text, looking at author bias or interpretation, documentation, and contemporary citation. While we may lament our students' relative indifference to such issues when we ask them to write their own research papers, if they are reading literary nonfiction on a topic that interests them, considering the sources and the basis of the work may be a way "in" to get students to care about these issues (and, again, Mark Twain's quotation at the beginning of this chapter may have strange pertinence here). What can we do?

- We can ask students to look at the point of view or even bias of the author: every writer has some sort of frame of reference; is that frame influencing the work?
- We can focus a discussion on source citations, currency of citations, and the difference between primary and secondary sources.
- We can look for language that may reveal an author's interpretation of events; what can students find?
- Some nonfiction speculates regarding the content of conversations not recorded and events not clearly established; can our students find instances of these, and are they legitimate in the context of the book? As a veteran teacher, you understand adolescents' fidelity to the concept of the truth (especially when it's the truth of others), and you can use this allegiance to deepen their interest in a piece of literary nonfiction.
- Some authors of creative nonfiction deliberately add fictive elements to their narratives in order to get at what they consider a deeper truth, to demonstrate a different perspective, or to emphasize a specific event. Can your students find these and determine whether the authors have achieved their purpose? Are there any limits to this form of creativity in literary nonfiction?

When we tout the "truth" of literary nonfiction, it is worthwhile considering what that truth may mean. Tim O'Brien fought in Vietnam and Elie Wiesel was imprisoned in a concentration camp; their experiences are part of the authority of their accounts, and while they are interpreting the events, they also lived them. Margot Lee Shetterly is writing of her family friends in *Hidden Figures*. But not all literary nonfiction is similarly situated, and thus our assessment of veracity can play out in fascinating ways in our study of literary nonfiction. After all, it's only relatively recently that we know that the classic of literary nonfiction, *The Diary of Anne Frank*, was heavily edited by Anne's father, Otto Frank, who did not wish certain passages to appear in the published work. Otto Frank did this for private family reasons, but it has skewed the full picture of Anne's thoughts and life, and the *Diary* most of us have read is incomplete, shaped, in a way, to someone else's truth. There are other examples, particularly in the area of memoir, where authors, mostly after publication, have admitted fabrication or extreme exaggeration of fact. (James Frey's *A Million Little Pieces* is one of the most notorious, as is Greg Mortenson and David Oliver Relin's *Three Cups of Tea* and, from some years back, Forrest Carter [Asa Earl Carter]'s *The Education of Little Tree*.)

So what is often touted as the "truth" of literary nonfiction is a bit less reliable than one might imagine. So verification of sources is one important issue. A standard practice of Susan Campbell Bartoletti is to use only primary sources that she has verified firsthand; for Bartoletti, secondary sources are unacceptable without this verification. Such work requires money to travel to archival sources and also time. Students could consider the implications of this kind of dedication—if, indeed, it is always necessary in all pieces of literary nonfiction, and if it is, what such dedication to truth does for the value of the work itself.

The author's stance can be crucial as well. For instance, Rebecca Skloot is white, and in *The Immortal Life of Henrietta Lacks* she details the ongoing discussions she had with the African American Lacks family and their mistrust of her as a white researcher and outsider to the family. In this case, as Skloot readily details, she herself became part of the Henrietta Lacks story, a witness, in a sense, to the painful legacy and sense of betrayal the family had endured after their mother and aunt Henrietta died. The importance/interference/insertion of the chronicler is not without precedent in literary nonfiction. Truman Capote was in a similar situation with the personal relationship he initiated with one of the main characters in *In Cold Blood,* generally considered the first "nonfiction novel." And in his 1999 *Dutch: A Memoir of Ronald Reagan*, Edmund Morris actually wrote himself as a character into the biography, upsetting historians with his novel approach.

How might any of these factors influence the truth of any account?

LINKING TO THE VISUAL

Another benefit of using literary nonfiction is its link to the visual; numerous books are also sources for video (multiple versions of *Anne Frank* as well as *The Glass Castle, Hidden Figures,* and *The Immortal Life of Henrietta Lacks* come to mind), including musical interpretations (the wildly successful Lin-Manuel Miranda Broadway hit based on *Alexander Hamilton*). Even graphic works are made into films, such as Marjane Satrapi's *Persepolis*. There are older films based on *In Cold Blood* and much documentary footage that could be related to *March, Hitler Youth, They Call Themselves the KKK,* and other works. Using clips from these visual works can complicate, enhance, and enliven literary nonfiction for students.

CONNECTING WITH OTHER CONTENT

Interdisciplinary studies at the middle and high school levels have taken a hit in this climate of testing, and your school may be one of many in which collaboration with other content teachers has taken a backseat. If there are links in place, however—or if you would like to establish such links—literary nonfiction is a fine way to connect with colleagues down the hall who are teaching science, history, and the arts. Perhaps co-written and co-taught curricula are a bridge too far, but cross-discussion and some coordination of what your students read in English and what they are doing in other classes can make for a powerful bridge between our literacy goals and those of other content areas. It can also breathe new life into a subject for a veteran teacher looking for something new. Bringing in your library media specialist may also help with this gap; it's something to move your teaching to the next level and to help your students see the strong connections between areas of study.

It's time for another trip to the Teachers' Lounge to find out more about what veteran teachers can do in the classroom with literary nonfiction. Our timing is excellent, as Lauren Leigh Kelly, a ten-year-plus English teaching veteran, is available to chat for a few minutes. Lauren is well known for incorporating hip-hop literacies into her teaching, and she recently completed a doctorate in English education. Today she's got some advice for us about engaging students in literary nonfiction by having them write oral histories.

FROM THE TEACHERS' LOUNGE

Digitally Documenting Oral Histories

Lauren Leigh Kelly
Rutgers University

I like an approach to writing literary nonfiction that involves cultivating skills in digital media literacy, critical listening, interviewing, and documenting oral histories. When I incorporate this in my classes, students conduct interviews with people they know from outside of the class and incorporate information from the interviews into their own personal narratives.

Here's my advice to my veteran colleagues for adding this rich literary nonfiction assignment into your classroom:

- *Begin by introducing the purpose and structure of personal narrative. Be sure to provide plenty of examples.*
- *Use brainstorming techniques such as time lines, memory mining, and writing prompts to help students choose a focus for their narrative.*
- *Next, tell your students they will experiment with writing a nonfiction account by interviewing someone they know (e.g., a friend, family member, teacher) about a particular moment or story in that person's life. (e.g., moving to the United States, becoming an accountant, etc.). The purpose of this initial interview is to prepare students to conduct future interviews deliberately designed to fuel their own personal narratives.*

- *Before the interviews, work with the students in class on creating open-ended and follow-up questions and listening with empathy.*
- *The interviews can be recorded through written notes, an audio recorder (recording apps can be found on most smartphones), or a combination of these.*
- *StoryCorps is an online resource that contains examples of oral histories and interviews between people who know each other. Take some time in class to introduce students to this website and to the diversity of stories it contains.*
- *After students have completed the interviews, they will submit a short narrative account of that person's story based on the interview. The narrative can be written from first person or third person point of view.*
- *At this point, students should have settled on the focus of their own narratives and have written a draft. They will then select a person (or more than one) who was a witness either to the event or to the time period the student is writing about. They will interview that person specifically about their perspective on that event or time period. (For example, if the narrative is about having difficulty in math class during sixth grade, a student can interview a friend who remembers what that student was like in sixth grade, or a family member who recalls the struggle.)*
- *In the final version of the personal narrative, the students will add another dimension to the story by incorporating the "outsider" perspective into the narrative. Students should have*

> *creative license to decide how they will do this; they might want to include quotes from the interview or create a section (distinguishable by italics, a subheading, or both) that is told from the first person point of view of the outsider.*

This process fosters empathy, builds stronger connections between students' lived spaces inside and outside of school, and reinforces the idea that our individual lives and stories are constantly interacting with, shaping, and being shaped by those of others.

FROM THE CLASSROOM

VIGNETTE: *THE THINGS THEY CARRIED*

Finally, we look at a classroom and one teacher's work with her students and a nonfiction classic. In early winter in a large, slightly overcrowded suburban high school, this "standard" class of twenty-three senior students is halfway through discussing Tim O'Brien's *The Things They Carried*. The fourteen males and nine females are mostly white (there are four students of color), and on this day their teacher asks the class to consider what, at this halfway point, "might change your minds" about their opinions of the book.

To focus the discussion, the teacher puts the students in groups of three and asks each student to take a piece of paper, fold it long ways, and write *Love* at the top. Students are to list ten items that come to mind associated with love; after about eight minutes and periodic checks on individuals, the teacher stops the students and asks them to share in their small group what they have listed. Students chat with one another.

The teacher then asks students to share and to talk as a whole: "Why did you choose that term?" starts off the discussion, but the teacher quickly turns to, "How do these emotions of love play out in *The Things They Carried*?" and "Can you elaborate on that?" The large-group discussion lasts approximately five minutes. Students are then asked to do the same with *War* as the focus: list ten items associated with the term, discuss in small groups, and then share as a whole.

In both segments, students are interested in talking, and each part of the discussion, *Love* and *War*, takes about twelve minutes total of classroom time for the two sets of listing, talking in small groups, and discussing in the large group.

But where does this lead in terms of "changing your mind" about *The Things They Carried*? For this teacher, the point is to look at both lists and consider what they have in common and what is different. Students are engaged in this contrast, and for a time they explore how the *Love* list is easier to create and discuss than that of *War*, even within the context of *The Things They Carried.* Students offer specific examples from the work to buttress the points, and when they are not forthcoming, the teacher asks for scenes as evidence. Students then move to fifteen minutes of silent reading of *Things* and consideration of a quotation from the work that deals with *both* love and war. After the reading, the class discussion resumes until the bell rings.

In this class and with these students, the teacher receives the kind of detailed responses she asks for, and at one point when students offer opinions that are divergent, she turns to quotations from the book and requests comments. She asks for a show of hands regarding opinions. "This is interesting to me," she notes at one point, and clearly it is also interesting to her students.

In a number of small ways, what this teacher does is effective, even exemplary. She:

- links student knowledge and opinion (what is love/ what is war?) to the work;
- sets up a structure for students to define two abstract values and then compare and contrast them;
- asks students to link the abstract values to the work being discussed;
- reinforces the use of evidence and specifics;
- uses different configurations and activities (individual work, small-group work, large-group discussion; listing, talking, reading);
- confirms to students that she is engaged by the student comments; and
- invites students to consider that their opinions may be shifting regarding *The Things They Carried.*

CONCLUSION

To crib from a biblical phrase, there are many mansions in the house of literature, and literary nonfiction is one of them. It can be a powerful genre for engaging our students, and its traditional basis of fact and truth makes its discussion and assessment something very different from that of fiction, poetry, and drama. Doug Hesse puts it well:

> If English classrooms have the reasonable aspiration to teach the reading and writing that students can or should encounter beyond our classrooms, then we ought to make a place for non-fiction written to delight and surprise, as well as texts meant transparently to contain "the point." (20)

The wide range of literary nonfiction can also appeal to students who are not that interested in the fictional events occurring in the streets of long-ago Verona, Italy, the difficulties of navigating the nineteenth-century Mississippi River, or the witch trials in Puritan-era Salem, Massachusetts. Literary nonfiction offers our students a broad look at the world, and today's bookstores and book clubs often feature literary nonfiction for the depth of insight and the lively discussion the genre engenders. Likewise, our classrooms can be strongly enhanced when we turn to literary nonfiction and use it consistently and well. In many ways, it opens new worlds to our students.

CHAPTER 5

Informational Texts: Harnessing the Power

Information is power only if you can take action with it.
Then, and only then, does it represent knowledge and, consequently, power.

—Daniel Burrus

Texts for which the primary purpose is the conveying of information have always been important parts of rich English classes, but with the onset of college- and career-readiness standards, informational texts are the recipients of significantly more emphasis. Like you, we believe it's important to increase middle and high school students' engagement with informational texts of all sorts. This is good news for us and our students because such texts are widely used in our society. Further, these texts have profound influence on each of us and on the world around us, and when we bring them into our classrooms, we bring with them the world. Veteran teachers are well positioned to skillfully use informational texts in the classroom.

THE POWER OF INFORMATIONAL TEXTS

Futurist and globally renowned business guru Daniel Burrus points out in the chapter epigraph the point that information on its own is not knowledge or power. Information becomes power only once someone takes some form of action with it. Burrus thus invites us to consider: are we doing all we can to help our students learn to understand, respond to, and *use* information in powerful and good ways? The answer to this question is an important one for us as English teachers.

Informational texts, even the most spare, direct, and possibly least interestingly written, can be important sources of knowledge that command significant control over students' lives (and ours, too). We owe it to students to help them be able to identify, understand, analyze, and apply informational texts effectively. Such texts underpin virtually every meaningful action that will affect a student's life and the life of the larger society. Informational texts are important for all literate citizens not just so they can contribute to the socioeconomics of the working world; there is also an important social justice element to teaching students to develop a critical literacy regarding informational texts. Just as poet Audre Lorde warns that "the master's tools will never dismantle the master's house," we acknowledge that many of the literacy tools of power are genres of informational text, and they can assert vast political and social power even in the guise of objective, apolitical statements. (Think of college financial aid policies, homeowner's association rules, reports of crime statistics, public opinion polls.) We empower students by helping them develop the ability to analyze and confront such texts and to purposefully wield informational text genres to support themselves and their causes. This is one of the worthiest—and possibly loftiest—of goals for our students and English classes.

THE APPEAL OF INFORMATIONAL TEXTS

As you may have noticed in your own classroom, many of our students actually prefer informational texts to fiction, drama, or poetry (just as they might prefer literary nonfiction to those genres) because they are inherently practical. Rather than inspiring flights of fancy or sharing abstract human experience (which, of course, we also value), informational texts directly fuel specific enterprises and help to solve particular problems. Informational texts also, by the way, help those budding creative writers in your classes enrich their imaginative texts with facts and details.

And there are other reasons right now to reassert the value of informational texts, particularly the importance of *credible* informational texts.

FACTS: AN ENDANGERED SPECIES?

Little in the recent past could have prepared any of us for what is now received wisdom regarding *fact.* As we also explore in Chapter 6, few of us could have imagined how powerful "fake news" and "alternative facts" have become. The 2016 US presidential election and its aftermath revealed how malleable, how fragile *facts* are when they are dismissed as just someone else's opinions. In a disturbing number of circles, widely accepted scientific laws are dismissed as theories, and crackpot conspiracy theories are given equal time with rigorously developed scientific hypotheses. Yesterday's snake oil salesmen have become today's "fake news" generators, spinning stories to stir people's passions and confirm their biases.

Contributing to these problems are the very tools we use to find facts: Internet search engines. As our browsers get better and better at helping us find the brands, blogs, and buys we like, so too do they direct us more and more narrowly toward the information we are most likely to embrace. Eli Pariser warned of the danger of what he called "filter bubbles" in his prescient 2011 TED Talk, "Beware Online 'Filter Bubbles.'" Facebook, Google, and other Internet forums use complex algorithms to edit the information on our screens without consulting us, Pariser points out. Another writer, Mostafa M. El-Bermawy, describes the Internet as an "echo chamber." He puts it strikingly: "The global village that was once the internet has been replaced by digital islands of isolation that are drifting further apart each day."

The dramatic increase in disinformation—false information that is deliberately created to hide the truth or to manipulate people's thoughts and actions—conspiring with our own literacy tools, has today endangered the very existence of "fact" as a concrete concept. If we are going to move into the future as an educated society, we must, while we still have the chance, reclaim the value of facts and prevent their extinction. Helping students understand, find, use, and especially *value* credible facts has become one of the most important jobs English teachers must do.

This is a highly significant set of issues. And when we feel a bit overwhelmed, we like to check in with colleagues. So let's take a walk to our ideal Teachers' Lounge. Lucky us! Thomas Newkirk—veteran teacher, former school board chair, and author of many beloved books, including *Minds Made for Stories: How We Really Read and Write Informational and Persuasive Texts*—is just getting himself a snack, and he has a few minutes to talk with us about the importance of teaching informational texts these days. For Tom, reading informational text is an ethical imperative.

FROM THE TEACHERS' LOUNGE

The Ethics of Informational Reading

Thomas Newkirk
University of New Hampshire, Emeritus

Informational reading is often viewed as a straightforward process—one of addition; we become better informed as we add to our stock of knowledge. Facts are good, hard things, and the more the better. Yet the great psychologist William James reminds us that we don't add a new fact "raw": "More usually it is embedded, cooked, as one might say, or stewed down in the sauce of the old" (75). In matters of belief, he reminds us, we are all conservatives, changing our core of knowledge and biases as little as possible.

The Language of Openness

I was surprised by . . .

It never occurred to me that . . .

I never realized what it was like to . . .

This changed the way I'm thinking about . . .

This tendency, pushed to an extreme, has been called "confirmation bias," the internal "yes man" in our consciousness that selects, deletes, and distorts information to accommodate preexisting opinions. For example, at the end of Barack Obama's presidency, 43 percent of Republicans believed that he was a Muslim (CNN), a "fact" that was manifestly untrue but consistent with a view of Obama as an outsider. Confirmation bias exists across the political spectrum. The truth, it often seems, is what you want to be the truth. Things are easier that way.

Which brings me to my insistence that reading informational texts is an ethical act, one in which we must monitor the tendency we all have to fit information into preexisting molds. It requires an openness to the new, the strange, the disconcerting; it requires a willingness to modify our pattern of sympathies and assumptions. It requires self-skepticism. And it affects what we read and how we read.

INFORMATIONAL TEXTS AT THE NEXT LEVEL

As a veteran teacher, you are already familiar with numerous genres of informational text, including how-to manuals, sets of directions, news articles, magazine feature stories, résumés and cover letters, even documentary films. But are you also bringing newer and more complex informational texts to your students? Let's look at a few you might want to use.

PRIMARY HISTORICAL DOCUMENTS

Documents, such as those found at the website of the Gilder Lehrman Institute of American History (www.gilderlehrman.org/collections) or at the Colorado Department of Education's World History Resources site (www.cde.state.co.us/cosocialstudies/worldhistoryresources), can add interest and insight to your class discussions. Students can be incredibly engaged when they experience genuine historical documents, as opposed to reading about those documents. See also Chadwick and Grassie, whose work provides great ideas for connecting historical documents to literary works.

CULTURAL STUDIES

Contemporary essays, reports, and critical examinations in cultural studies, such as those found at the New York University (NYU) Center for Latin American and Caribbean Studies website (http://clacs.as.nyu.edu/object/clacs.k12outreach.curricularmaterials), are also well worth exploring. These materials can be especially helpful for broadening the experiences of all your students and for encouraging English language learners to bring their experiences to your class.

TECHNICAL DOCUMENTS

Reports that include charts, graphs, maps, and other visuals will greatly broaden your students' literacy skills. The Bureau of Labor Statistics has a wealth of such resources (www.bls.gov/home.htm), including an interesting Chart Maker tool (www.bls.gov/k12/content/students/chart-maker/chart-maker.htm). The PEW Research Center's site (www.pewresearch.org/topics/) includes a list of their research reports on dozens of topics, including reports on American trends, Asian Americans, gay marriage and homosexuality, online gaming, poverty, and dozens more. Gallup (http://www.gallup.com) has also published scores of reports and blogs on politics, education, economics, and well-being across the globe. Encourage students to complete research using Google Forms or a similar platform that allows individuals to collect data in a variety of interesting formats and also provides colorful analytics.

PODCASTS

Add to your curriculum podcasts, such as those offered by National Public Radio, *The Economist,* the Smithsonian Institution, and just about any other major news source or museum out there. The auditory medium has experienced a resurgence with the availability of Internet streaming. Part of our responsibility is to help our students understand how to approach these texts using critical thinking.

WORKPLACE DOCUMENTS

Real workplace correspondence, such as memos; brief reports; PowerPoint, Google Slides, or Prezi presentations; and emails may not sound particularly interesting (though they can be), but they will certainly contribute to an atmosphere of credibility and relevance in your classroom. We believe that students' first experiences with these genres should occur long before they earn a paycheck. Workplace correspondence matters, and students should see how communication contributes to an organization's mission—and to an individual's salary and well-being.

SOCIAL MEDIA

Social media has virtually exploded onto the communication scene and has quickly globalized interaction. New genres—including texts, tweets, blogs, comments, status updates, and the many variations on these depending on the newest platforms and trends—are all forms of communication that today's students must learn to read rigorously. Ready or not, social media continues its enormous impact on the world. Giving these discourses short shrift in English class allows these texts to manipulate students for the rest of their lives. (See Chapter 6 for a closer look at social media texts.)

REFERENCE AND POLICY MANUALS

Do your students know how to use an American English usage manual (Garner is terrific!) and a grammar handbook? Do they know how to find correct information from credible sources of fact on the Internet? Are they acquainted with the school's student honor code, or the student conduct handbook from the local college, or the employee handbook from a large local business? These are also nonfiction texts with which our students should become comfortable.

ADVERTISEMENTS

Commercials and advertisements have long been staples in some English classes. Ever since William Lutz's 1989 *Doublespeak*, teachers have engaged students in close reading of the use of manipulative language, particularly to sell products. Now there are other genres students should be reading closely: pop-up ads (integrated into browsers and powered by cookies) and infographics, which use dazzling data visualization techniques to sell information (for good, ill, or otherwise). While explaining how to have students create their own infographics is beyond the scope of this text, check out Lindblom et al. for more information.

COURT DECISIONS

When US Supreme Court decisions appear in the news, use the occasion to encourage students to read what judges write in their decisions. The prose can be very high level, and often the rulings address timely issues that are occasionally fascinating and even important to daily life. FindLaw (caselaw.findlaw.com/) is a helpful free resource for local, state, and US Supreme Court case documents.

US LAWS

A society is made peaceable and manageable through the laws it follows. When appropriate, encourage students to examine the real language that regulates their lives. USA.gov (www.usa.gov/laws-and-regulations) is an excellent source for current laws and policies at the federal level, and it includes links to state laws on particular topics.

STUDENTS AS SOURCES OF INFORMATIONAL TEXT

Finally, don't forget to ask your students about their interests and to seek their help in bringing interesting informational texts to class. Just as in a fiction reading workshop, we can harness the power of students' literacy to create a library of worthwhile texts. Consider allowing the fiction, poetry, and drama you already read in your classroom to inspire searches for informational text.

So, are you reading *The Taming of the Shrew*? Look up the history of marriage laws. Reading *To Kill a Mockingbird*? Find an essay about how a trial is supposed to work to render justice, or explore news articles that cover a recent racially charged trial. If *The Great Gatsby* is on your list, see what information PEW or Gallup has available about wealth distribution and culture. If you're planning to assign *The Catcher in the Rye*, find a good source for mental health care issues and options for young people.

For Leila, informational text often comes from unfamiliar sources, and in one case, she was humbled by the excellence of informational text.

AS AN ADEPT READER *and English teacher, I feel happy in the world of words, and bringing to students just about any kind of text has generally been well within my comfort zone. What helps me break out and stretch beyond this kind of complacency, however, is a short stroll in informational text. In most cases, the texts I prefer to use are routinely featured in publications with which I am not familiar.*

Consider the opening three sentences of a recent article in Autoweek, *a newsmagazine characterized by high-level writing and research:*

> *Even before General Motors declared bankruptcy in 2009, it was wrestling with the choice to ditch the Hummer brand. This wasn't all Hummer's fault, but with its aggressive design, military heritage and unapologetic profligacy, it had become something of a toxic asset in a world beset by a wildly unpopular hawk president, an interminable war and escalating fuel prices amid global economic collapse. The real problem, though, was with GM. (Berk 11)*

Informational texts such as this are eye-opening to students and to us as teachers; this kind of writing, possibly on a topic with which we are not familiar, demonstrates excellent prose craft—inventive phrasing, a high-level vocabulary, use of detail, and creative alteration of sentence length. For students who might be interested in or knowledgeable about a certain kind of vehicle, in this case the Hummer, this passage can be a particularly appealing model to use for writing and for packing facts into a short space. In my teaching of informational texts, I turn to journals such as Autoweek*. In the case of "Brash. Vulgar. Extinct.," I'm not really interested in driving or buying a Hummer, but I know a lot more than I did about the vehicle, its history, and its future. Further, I am more than awed by the quality of the informational writing.*

Let's now look at another classroom to see how one teacher has had her students create informational text.

FROM THE CLASSROOM

VIGNETTE: CREATING INFORMATIONAL TEXT

In February in this mixed suburban/rural middle school, the English 8 class begins at 8:15 a.m. The classroom is located in a late-century modern school building, and the seventeen girls and eleven boys in English 8 are largely white (as is their female teacher), with five students of color.

Their topic of study is a huge one, globalization, and students in small groups have been allowed to select under this umbrella topic specific areas of interest. The student groups have chosen and researched within a wide array of areas, including refugees, water pollution, poverty, hunger, and global warming.

This morning is the culmination of the multiweek globalization unit, which has extended through four class periods, including a library trip or two. Students have explored and recorded their findings, and today, in a visual bazaar, the final projects are displayed in stations posted all around the classroom.

Now, after thirty minutes of opening announcements and the Pledge of Allegiance, instructions and distribution of materials, and final confirmation of projects, the students get out of their chairs to circumnavigate the classroom. Using a chart form and check sheet, they visit each final project display. There are multiple projects, but the movement of the students is organized and orderly, and as students circulate they are asked to answer on their chart two questions, *What is the project's message? What are two facts I learned?,* and, giving specific reasons, to indicate on their chart their vote (with reasons) for the best project. In eight-minute increments, the teacher calls time and paces the students so that each project is viewed in turn and receives its full amount of scrutiny.

The noise level is relatively high, but clearly it's because the students are serious about this evaluation. One of the major challenges of these eight-minute project viewings is that this teacher has encouraged students to present their information (with bibliography) in a variety of informational text forms: project results and research are represented through student-created TED Talks; public service announcements (PSAs); T-shirts; CD covers; traditional news articles; poems; and children's picture books. At a number of project stations, laptops are required for the TED Talks and the PSAs and, in one case, a student's phone is used.

Among the twenty-eight students in this class, most of these options have been explored, particularly the TED Talks, PSAs, and T-shirts, and the projects displayed demonstrate the range of how crucial facts can be presented using different media.

The seriousness of the students as they assess is clear, and for sixty minutes of class time, discussion of these projects and their assessment is paramount. At the end of the hour, students turn in their completed charts with their notes and votes. During class the next day, all projects will be discussed and the winner revealed.

What happens in this English 8 class is noteworthy and, in its own way, exemplary. Centering the unit on informational research, the teacher has:

- selected a broad topic of contemporary and even compelling interest;
- encouraged students to pursue a more manageable subtopic so that they have some investment in the research;
- provided a range of ways for students to present their information, including new media such as TED Talks, PSAs, and even T-shirts; and
- used student expertise and specific evaluative criteria to assess the projects.

The power of informational text can be brought home when students are allowed to create their own; in this class in this middle school, an organized teacher and willing students have created new knowledge and understandings of a large and complex topic. Through this project, research skills have been reinforced, appreciation of an abstract concept has been enhanced, and students have created their own informational texts.

Reading all these possibilities makes us wonder about other resources. We bet there's someone in our Teachers' Lounge who also might have some ideas. Sure enough, Amy Jo Southworth, veteran high school English teacher and now librarian in the Bay Shore Schools in New York, has some excellent suggestions.

FROM THE TEACHERS' LOUNGE

A Librarian Helps You Find Just the Informational Texts You're Looking For!

Amy Jo Southworth
Mary G. Clarkson Elementary School, Bay Shore, New York

School and public librarians are positioned to assist in the location of informational texts and in the interpretation and use of various text features in the classroom. Librarians regularly access databases that curate current and authoritative materials. These resources are a part of the "deep" or "invisible Web" and not accessible through basic Google searches. Librarians can teach students and teachers to navigate these sources in order to locate the most appropriate items. Teaching students such skills is fundamental information literacy and is invaluable in an era of "fake news."

The websites of respected organizations like the Library of Congress and Smithsonian's TweenTribune offer extensive collections and maintain standards-based, discipline-specific lesson databases, Lexile levels, and teacher guides. Outstanding websites include Newsela, Wonderopolis, CommonLit, and DOGOnews. Google News Archive and Newseum offer comprehensive, international newspaper content.

It is also important to consider visuals, including infographics, as informational text. Credible sites like the Pew Research Center offer excellent materials as well as databases.

Informational texts lend themselves to close reading—a technique used to teach students to authentically engage with documents. Examining these texts can help make students aware of where information comes from *and how it comes* to us. *Close reading can also mean studying the unique and complex features of informational texts, including print features, organizational aids, keywords, diagrams, and various changes in font that impact meaning.*

How we approach informational text also makes an important difference in student learning. If students choose a text, they have a much higher level of engagement. Authentic reasons for reading also help: create assignments that require students to use informational texts to solve real-world problems or mysteries. Most important, work beside students to acknowledge the potential difficulty and ultimate importance of making the effort to engage with credible information.

INTEGRATING INFORMATIONAL TEXTS

So, having identified informational texts of various genres, and if we agree about the importance of helping students develop a critical literacy specific to informational texts, how do we proceed in our classrooms? What follows is our advice on finding better ways to critically examine informational texts (e.g., articles, reports, studies). We also want to provide some advice regarding better integration of informational texts of all types into your existing curriculum.

APPROACHING INFORMATIONAL TEXTS

Reading informational text is not the same as reading other forms of text. Frequently, it's best to read informational pieces by first getting an overview of the entire piece, determining its shape and purpose before diving into a full reading of the text from beginning to end. One of Ken's most popular lessons is a simple one in which he talks out loud as he reads, in this case as he approaches a new research article. This is a teacher "performing" meta-thinking:

SO I HAVE A NEW *article here from* College English, *a research journal devoted to teaching English that I read often. First I look at the title and the author, and I think about the other works I know that cover this topic and other research that I know this author has written. I then read the abstract, paying particular attention to the findings section, because I want to know where this article gets to before I decide to devote my time to reading it closely. Now I turn to the works cited section, checking to see which scholars and traditions this writer is drawing on. This will tell me pretty quickly if this author is going to say something I can understand and respect, if the topic is well known to me. If I don't know the topic well, I read the article titles and journal names carefully to learn more about the knowledge this article is drawing on. What lines of inquiry are likely to be made? What knowledge base will this article contribute to? As a next step, I start to read all the subtitles in the article. If it's a traditional study, I will look quickly to see what methods the author is using to gather and interpret data, and I will look more closely at discussions of findings. If there are charts or graphs, I might take a quick look, but I'm more likely to hunt for explanatory text (which is my own preference as a reader). If it's not a traditional study, I'll read the subtitles more carefully, and perhaps the first and last few sentences of*

each section, to get a sense of the shape of the article. Once I think I know what the author's intention is and I think I have a good sense of how the argument will build (and where it's going), I may choose to invest the time necessary to read it from beginning to end. Of course, even if I do read it all, I may skim some sections. If it's an article that really compels me—because I'm invested in the topic or because I may want to use it in my own writing—I will read it fully and multiple times.

Ken finds that his students appreciate being told explicitly that not all texts should be read the same way, and that it's okay to skim. In fact, at a certain point skimming becomes a necessity, given how much reading is often necessary. Students also really seem to like having someone talk right in front of them about how they are reading a complicated piece, what most teachers term a *talk-aloud protocol*. Elementary teachers do this all the time for new readers, and we middle-level and secondary teachers can take note. When the texts require a new way of reading or require a more sophisticated approach than just starting at the beginning, a talk-aloud protocol can be effective.

It may be unlikely that middle and high school students would be reading full-blown research articles, but it's still perfectly fine for teachers to demonstrate how they read the works in their field. *Voices from the Middle* or *English Journal* would be excellent journals to use. If you want to incorporate student-friendly works, they also are out there. For example, check out *Environmental Science Journal for Kids* (www.sciencejournalforkids.org/), an online journal that presents peer-reviewed research in a concise and engaging format. Articles include abstracts, methods sections, references, and more, so teachers can use them to model how reading an informational piece is different from reading a literary work.

A really fun way to discuss the features of a research article is to use a text called—we kid you not—"Chicken Chicken Chicken: Chicken Chicken" (Zongker). This is a six-page research article that includes six subsections with titles, a table, two graphs, two flowcharts, and a works cited section. And every single word of the text is *chicken*. (It's a quick read, but it's likely to make you hungry or homesick, depending on your relationship to chickens.) Apparently the article was originally intended by a graduate student at the University of Washington (now a Google engineer) as a parody of jargon-laden, overly complex research writing. It did that well. But we also find that it's a great tool for encouraging students to look at the rhetorical elements of a research text without getting bogged down in the details of the prose. We don't have enough time to go into detail about how to use "Chicken Chicken Chicken: Chicken Chicken" to keep your students abreast of informational text features, but you should be plucky enough to wing it. You may find you have a leg up on your colleagues. (Sorry, but we couldn't resist.)

Engaging young students in informational reading can be especially challenging. Our colleague Sharon Hinkson has been teaching for several years in a large suburban district with students from a wide range of socioeconomic and cultural backgrounds. We knew she would have excellent advice about teaching informational literacy to junior high students. Luckily, Sharon has a few minutes to spend with us in the Teachers' Lounge before she runs off to her next class.

FROM THE TEACHERS' LOUNGE

Informational Texts in Middle Grades

Sharon Hinkson

Longwood Junior High School, Middle Island, New York

If you're like me and you teach the middle grades, you know that informational text reading usually gets the eye roll from students. The technicality of informational texts proves to be challenging at the middle level, particularly if you have struggling readers and bilingual students. Regardless of how students may feel about informational text reading, it is a skill set they need for their future as students and in their careers.

How, then, can we get students engaged in this type of reading? I find that middle school students still want the "story." Therefore, supplying informational texts that have an element of story in them is like offering a glass of vinegar with a honey chaser.

I've tried a number of things, but I've had success introducing challenging material through a comprehensive video on the topic we're studying that children at their level can relate to. I also find very helpful simply reading the text aloud to my students and then backtracking with questions about what I've just read and/or—even better—relating a personal story that is somehow connected to the text. After my students have a general idea what the text is about, which I determine by assessing our small-group and whole-class discussions, I direct the students to go through the text highlighting words they are unfamiliar with, researching the definitions, and annotating their copy with the definition. In a class that will undoubtedly have a range of proficiencies, some students will derive the meaning of terms from context clues, while others will need a dictionary and further explanations.

There are no easy answers here. We must know our students' capabilities and find fun, interesting ways to help our students digest informational texts.

DEVELOPING RESPECT FOR CREDIBLE INFORMATION

We alluded earlier to the idea that facts are becoming a beleaguered—if not endangered—species. For some critics of today's discourse, once rigorous social and political argument has atrophied into repeated claims that appear to have little relation to truth and no apparent connection to the claims made by others involved in the discussion. For today's pessimists—and there are plenty of them around—the state of logical, credible, ethical argument in this country is abysmal. And, like it or not, we veteran teachers share some responsibility for the present situation. Every single American basing decisions on bias rather than logic, "fake news" rather than factual reporting, disinformation rather than credibly-sourced accounts, has had a series of English teachers. As a profession, we have an obligation to do better.

The ancient rhetoric teacher Quintilian emphasized the need for teachers to create *the good man speaking well*. Quintilian's call to us is to teach our students to be ethical people, using the rhetorical skills we help them develop for purposes they consider good for the world. Perhaps we can't ensure that all of our students are ethical thinkers, but we can certainly engage them in repeated and rigorous critical discussions that engage them in understanding the value of truth, informed perspectives, and ethically minded speculation; the importance of appropriately qualified claims; and the impact on others of well-founded argument. These activities can help:

- Ensure your students understand and have experience identifying and avoiding logical fallacies. A quick Internet search can reveal brief, simple lists or incredibly complicated and sophisticated information about fallacious logic.
- Let students study some real-world results of bad information. Corruption, greed, sloppiness, and more have inspired bad information and results. Help students learn from others' examples why it's important to develop a preference for true, credible information.
- Teach your students to debate properly, responding to one another's points firmly but politely rather than engaging in ad hominem attacks or a series of statements that don't truly interact with each other. Use "debates" on television to demonstrate nonrigorous debating; there's no shortage of examples. Invite your school's debate or forensics coach to speak with your class about classic debate and its rules and format.
- Help students closely analyze informational texts so they can see how a complex argument builds, addressing counterarguments along the way. Have students write up claims and evidence on cards and then physically move the claims and informa-

tion around to better understand how effective arguments are built, as Patricia A. Dunn suggests. See her "Rhetorical Proof Cards" (available free on the Heinemann website). Find "Cards" in her *Talking, Sketching, Moving: Multiple Literacies in the Teaching of Writing* (60–65).

- Encourage your students to pay very close attention to how information and argumentation move through social media. The range and rate of information has always been at the speed of the Internet, as far as our students are concerned. Veteran teachers have to understand social media (e.g., tweets, status updates, memes, blogs) well enough to help our students read it and react to it responsibly. (See Chapter 6 for much more information on social media.)

Educating people to speak or write accurately, fairly, and well is a challenge for all of us. We must work together as a field to increase our efforts in support of this goal. With the rapid expanse and speed of information brought about by the Internet and social media, this challenge has never been more daunting or more important. We veteran teachers must meet it head on.

READING INFORMATIONAL TEXTS WITH PURPOSE

In the world outside school, it is rare for anyone to read an informational text simply for pleasure. In general, people approach informational texts with a reason, an authentic purpose. So it's important for us to ensure our students have genuine purposes for reading informational texts and to assist them in developing the reading processes needed to achieve those purposes.

In the world beyond school, readers use informational texts to learn about health care options, get legal advice, file their taxes, improve their skills, develop hobbies, make better meals, decide whether or not to see a particular movie or buy a particular album, apply for a gun license, gain employment, make big purchases, learn to play a new game, and so on. What purposes can we devise for students to read informational texts in our English classes?

Consider the following:

- Could you ask students to look up interesting statistics about their favorite athlete, actor, or writer?
- How would students react to skimming articles to find important details about or perspectives on a local event that has attracted attention?
- What about scouring the Internet for informational sources that present solutions to a problem at your school: bullying, overtesting, contentious social issues, lack of school spirit, underfunding of school-related activities?
- Would it be interesting to students to explore details, statistics, historical facts about the town or the neighborhood they live in, or about any prominent members of the community?
- Is there a local industry that has had (or continues to have) an economic, environmental, or social impact on the community that students could research?
- Could students read about future careers or college majors or find information about and advice for creating wealth? Or pursuing volunteerism?

Many of today's students are interested in getting involved in the community. Teachers can harness that energy into literacy projects that require real reading and research and can result in real action. To give one example, Heidi Hallman's students, at the time either pregnant and/or parenting teens, were outraged by an insulting letter to the local newspaper editor about the program that educates them. Hallman helped her students channel their anger into a series of written responses, all of which, to make an effective case, required reading and research. Similarly, Kim-Marie Cortez-Riggio's students researched and wrote detailed pamphlets highlighting important local environmental issues.

These are just two real-world examples. As a veteran teacher, you know that encouraging students to engage in authentic research has its risks, especially if students are going to present their results beyond the classroom. But authentic assignments have such benefits for the students and their community that it's arguably well worth the risk, and veteran teachers can negotiate that risk effectively. Positive school-community relations can also build from such student work and research, and these days that's as important as it's ever been.

Ideas like these are exciting and inspiring. But where can we go for more examples and in-depth advice about creating and teaching our students the details of authentic research? Time to consult our colleagues in the Teachers' Lounge. Right now, Lisa Storm Fink is there. Lisa is the long-time project manager for the rich and expansive ReadWriteThink database. For years Lisa has worked with NCTE to develop creative and rigorous lesson plans and other resources that teachers can use for free. She's got some excellent suggestions for mining the site for ideas about teaching informational texts.

FROM THE TEACHERS' LOUNGE

NCTE and ReadWriteThink Resources for Your Classroom

Lisa Storm Fink
National Council of Teachers of English

Don't forget to use NCTE as a source of quality informational texts. The NCTE Orbis Pictus Award promotes and recognizes excellence in the writing of nonfiction for children. The name Orbis Pictus commemorates the work of Johannes Amos Comenius, Orbis Pictus—The World in Pictures *(1657), considered to be the first book actually planned for children. See these award-winning and honor books at http://bit.ly/2qSfNEc. NCTE also has a rich archive of resources, from journal articles and blog posts to podcasts and webinars that can be found by simply searching the NCTE site (www.ncte.org).*

Once you've made informational texts available and accessible to your students in a class library, spend some time acquainting students with the genre. Use these texts as part of an interactive read-aloud.

Engage students in discussion about the text features, structure, and organization, and make connections or comparisons to other texts. Learn more about interactive read-alouds with this ReadWriteThink (RWT) strategy guide: http://bit.ly/13ldXOM. Then move to a guided reading of informational texts as you step students up to independently reading informational texts during class time and after.

These days it's imperative that students learn how to critically approach digital informational content. Teachers of all disciplines can work together to teach students how to determine the accuracy, currency, and reliability of materials from various sources. Students should also learn to choose and analyze information sources for individual, academic, and functional purposes. Learn more with the RWT lesson plan "Research Building Blocks: Examining Electronic Sources," which is part of a larger unit on research: http://bit.ly/2bG1Rsu. It's designed for younger students, but veteran teachers can easily adapt it for more sophisticated readers.

Many informational texts are presented visually, both in print and online. Students of all grade levels must be able to interpret infographics, charts, maps, and graphs. Often these graphics contain information not included in the text. Teachers should work with students on how to read graphics as well as text, using modeling, scaffolding, and other reading comprehension techniques. "A Picture IS Worth a Thousand Words: Using Infographics to Illustrate How-to Writing" engages students in a genre that combines graphics and text: http://bit.ly/1TI3lOz.

Making sure that your classroom is rich with informational texts helps students learn about the world around them. This builds their content knowledge, which can influence their ability to make sense of other texts while also increasing their knowledge about the world. Please remember that NCTE's and ReadWriteThink's resources are always just a few clicks away.

INCORPORATING INFORMATIONAL TEXTS INTO TEXT SETS

It's a good idea to align your assignments of informational texts into larger sets of texts that you have selected based on a theme. Creating a unit around an essential question with a variety of textual entry points is an excellent way to engage students' interest and approach the topic with depth and nuance. Text sets are nothing new, but selecting and aligning mindfully is an important skill for veteran teachers to continually develop and employ in their planning. When developing a thematic unit, teachers should consider the full range of literacy skills, content knowledge, and dispositions they intend for students to build from the unit. Veteran teachers must take their teaching of informational texts to the next level by carefully identifying a variety of informational texts and mindfully integrating them into broader units of study focused on engaging and substantial learning outcomes. This usually also includes integrating literary and informational texts. How do we do this?

One of our favorite strategies for planning integration of informational texts comes from Sarah Brown Wessling's formulation of a "fulcrum text" with "context texts" and "texture texts," the definitions of each (and the relationships between them) explained best in Figure 5.1, Wessling's graphic from *Supporting Students in a Time of Core Standards: English Language Arts, Grades 9–12* (27). Although it's possible to select an informational text to serve as a fulcrum, it's more likely that informational texts, particularly brief or complicated technical documents, would better serve as shorter context or texture texts to support a fiction or literary nonfiction book.

In Table 5.1, Wessling lists "informative texts" as those to select for context or texture texts, but she doesn't provide examples (24). We suggest use of the following: scientific studies, statistical surveys, primary historical documents, legislation or judicial decisions (all of which can be found in the databases listed earlier in the chapter), short theoretical or philosophical treatises, op-eds and editorials, news articles or magazine features, personal interviews, and more. Planning a mix of text types on a similar theme can create a structure from which many absorbing, relevant, and rigorous literacy lessons can be constructed.

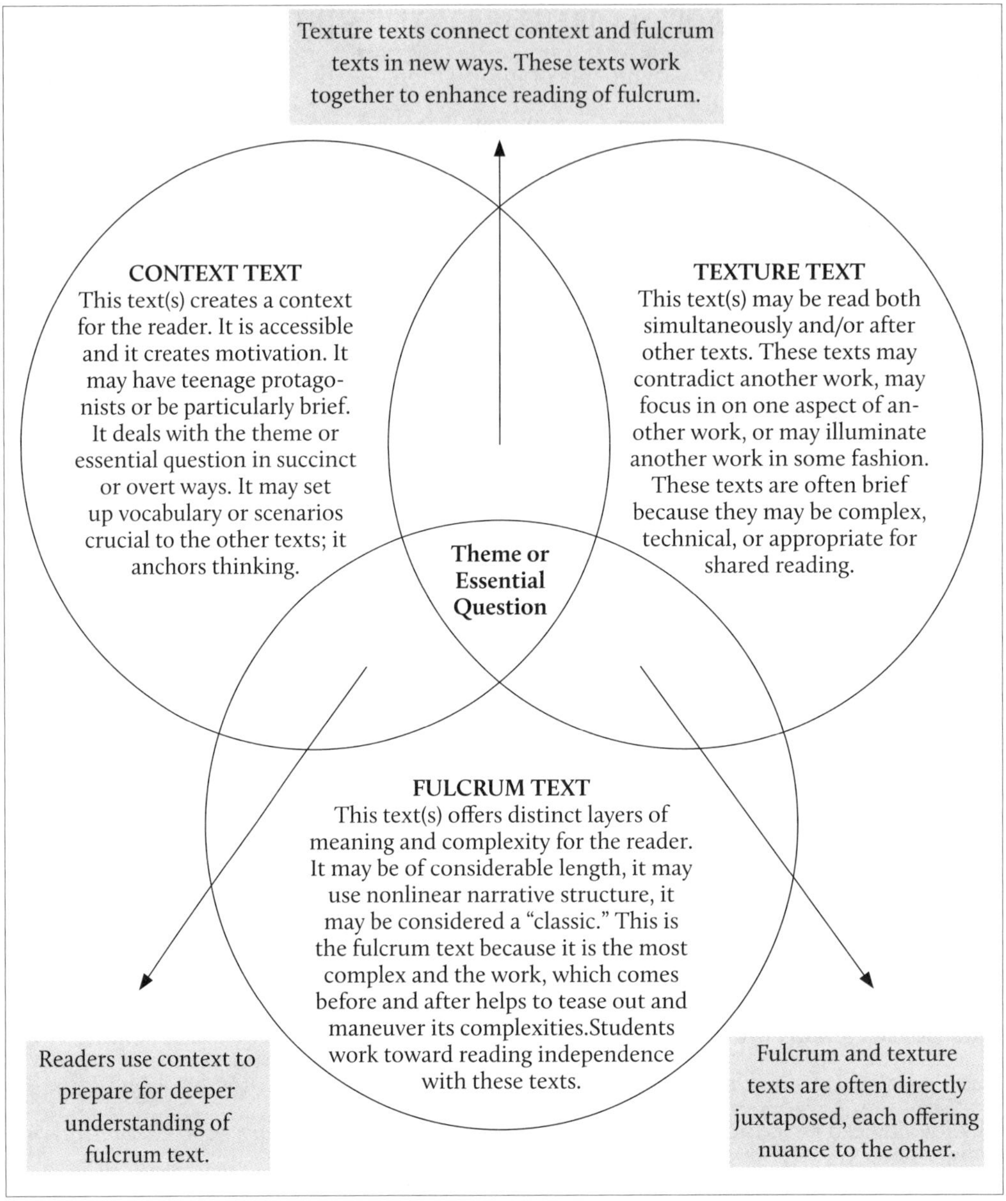

FIGURE 5.1. Sarah Brown Wessling's reading complexity circles.

Table 5.1. Sarah Brown Wessling's List of Sample Texts for Reading Complexity Circles

Context texts *These accessible "anchor" texts create a reservoir of prior knowledge that gives context to the complexity of further reading.*	**Fulcrum texts** *These texts are often the traditional whole-class text or they take the place of that whole-class text.*	**Texture texts** *While these texts often seem to be shorter, it also is effective to juxtapose two major texts to create reading texture.*
film film excerpts informative pieces news/magazine articles blog radio show podcast short story poetry drama young adult literature brief fiction brief nonfiction graphic novel	book-length fiction book-length nonfiction short story or stories drama poem or series of poems film student selected text whole-class text	film film excerpts informative pieces news/magazine articles blog radio show podcast short story poetry drama young adult literature brief fiction brief nonfiction graphic novel

This talk is good advice in theory, but how does a teacher really do it? In the following section, we create a thematic text set inspired by Jay Asher's *Thirteen Reasons Why*.

PLANNING A THEMATIC UNIT FROM A RANGE OF TEXT TYPES: *THIRTEEN REASONS WHY*

Jay Asher published *Thirteen Reasons Why* in 2007, but it became a focus of national discussion due to a 2017 serial dramatization of it on Netflix. A book written for young people about a teen's suicide would likely be controversial in any case, but the Netflix series raised significant concerns among some for what is seen as a potential romanticization of suicide and the in-depth and solitary viewing that streaming can provide; that is, some worry about young people watching all thirteen episodes at once without anyone else there to talk with about this weighty topic. Many people deal with suicidal thoughts or with the aftermath of a real suicide. It's not a pleasant topic, to say the least, but it's one a veteran teacher can take up respectfully and responsibly in the context of a literacy unit. *Thirteen Reasons Why* also raises a series of other social issues, including bullying, sexual assault, invasion of privacy, stalking, the stakes of friendship, and more, all of which are of interest to teens and topics they, unfortunately, should learn about. And we can provide responsible settings for those topic discussions. Below we recommend texts for a unit, using Asher's book as the fulcrum text, as an example of a way to incorporate real-world informational texts into the ELA classroom.

SELECTING THE TEXTS AND TEXT TYPES

The Fulcrum Text. *Thirteen Reasons Why* will serve as our center, and we will read the book throughout the entire unit. The novel is a fairly short and relatively simple read. The topics of the text, however, are emotional and complicated; it's important for readers to discuss the text as they read to ensure they understand the plot, follow the connotations, and don't misinterpret the text as a glorification of suicide or an invitation to take revenge on those who bully. We will incorporate a range of other texts and text types as context texts or texture texts, as described next.

Context Texts. These texts are intended to help students be *ready* to learn what they will learn from the fulcrum text. In this case, the fulcrum text is not a complicated read, so the students won't need much help understanding the theme and plot, but they will require background and understanding to get a sense of the issues that arise throughout the text. We plan to use context texts to incorporate scientific studies, information about social issues from books and magazines, statistics that can inform us about the impact of these problems, and information about how people can find and offer help.

For our context texts, we will choose among the following:

- "Common Views and Myths about Bullying," a two-page handout from Pacer's National Bullying Prevention Center (www.pacer.org/publications/bullypdf/BP-1.pdf).
- The Pew Research Center's "Cyberbullying 2010: What the Research Tells Us" (www.pewinternet.org/2010/05/06/cyberbullying-2010-what-the-research-tells-us/) is a report that delivers useful information (in text, statistics, and chart form) about teens' online habits, as well as the definition and effects of cyberbullying. Since this research is from 2010 (half a lifetime ago for today's high schoolers), students can engage in a conversation to update some of the facts listed.
- The US Centers for Disease Control and Prevention (CDC) has a great deal of information on suicide. This chart shows the leading causes of death among people of various ages: www.cdc.gov/injury/images/lc-charts/leading_causes_of_death_age_group_2014_1050w760h.gif. Suicide ranks second highest among those ten to thirty-four years old.
- The CDC also has a site that includes risk factors and protective factors regarding suicide, and additional resources for help: www.cdc.gov/violenceprevention/suicide/riskprotectivefactors.html.
- Teen romance (gone right and wrong) is an important plot element in *Thirteen Reasons Why* and in your students' young lives. Monica Anderson's "Digital Romance: How Teen Boys and Girls Differ" may lend an air of reality to your students' reading of the novel: www.pewresearch.org/fact-tank/2015/10/13/digital-romance-how-teen-boys-and-girls-differ/.
- DeSilver's "Dangers That Teens and Kids Face: A Look at the Data" (www.pewresearch.org/fact-tank/2016/01/14/dangers-that-young-people-face-a-look-at-the-data) is a sobering account of the problems teens may encounter, several of which are highlighted in *Thirteen Reasons Why*. The full text or just an excerpt of this online article might be appropriate for this unit, depending on our students.

- Given the negativity of some of these context texts, it might also be a good idea to include something that shows young people taking a positive stand against bullying. The NPR story (available in text and in audio form) "Teen Creates App So Bullied Kids Never Have to Eat Alone" is about a student who created an app to help lonely students find schoolmates to eat lunch with: www.npr.org/sections/thesalt/2016/09/15/494074992/teen-creates-app-so-bullied-kids-never-have-to-eat-alone.

Texture Texts. Adding different text types (genres other than young adult fiction) that relate directly to the themes of *Thirteen Reasons Why* will enhance the depth of thought and discussion we have as a class about the book, and about text and literacy more generally. Adding different kinds of texts will also add "texture," as Wessling's term denotes, to students' literacy skills. Here we would include clips from the Netflix production of the book, provocative paintings and other works of art that bring nuance to the topic, and newspaper articles that give factual accounts that echo in some way the events of the book. Here are some of the resources we will choose from:

- "To This Day" is a poem by Shane Koyczan set to a seven-minute video, available at www.youtube.com/watch?v=ltun92DfnPY. Rich in emotion and metaphor and ending on a positive note, the poem is a powerful enhancement of many themes and plot points in *Thirteen Reasons Why*. Even better, Koyczan recorded a twelve-minute TED Talk in which he speaks the poem and gives additional background and context on it, providing a more informational text: www.ted.com/talks/shane_koyczan_to_this_day_for_the_bullied_and_beautiful/transcript?language=en.
- Stopbullying.gov has a site (www.stopbullying.gov/cyberbullying/what-is-it/index.html) that includes several very short videos that students might find intriguing enough to prompt them to examine the genre of the short video, a text type that is quickly becoming a staple of informational text.

- Gallup's "Parents' School Safety Fears Haven't Receded since Newtown" (www.gallup.com/poll/164168/parents-school-safety-fears-haven-receded-newtown.aspx?g_source=bullying&g_medium=search&g_campaign=tiles) can enlighten students about parents' concerns about their children's safety in school. Interestingly, this survey indicates that students are less concerned than their parents.
- The sad events of *Thirteen Reasons Why* are, unfortunately, inspired by real-world incidents. This short NPR story (print only) details the punishments received by two young women after a third woman they bullied committed suicide: www.npr.org/sections/thetwo-way/2013/10/15/235104253/felony-charges-for-2-in-suicide-of-bullied-girl. The *New York Times* also reports on the crime, allowing students to examine contrasts between the accounts: www.nytimes.com/2013/10/16/us/felony-charges-for-2-girls-in-suicide-of-bullied-12-year-old-rebecca-sedwick.html?hp.
- "Youth-Powered Social Cause Takes Shape in the Form of 'Bully Project'" is a site that includes several pieces of artwork designed to raise the problem of bullying, and also includes information about the docudrama *Bully*: www.psfk.com/2014/11/adobe-anti-bullying-project-mural-street-artists.html.
- Finally, we would include more information from PACER's National Anti-Bullying Center: a two-page handout titled "Drama: Is It Happening to You? Advice for Teens Who Are Experiencing Bullying" (www.pacer.org/publications/bullypdf/BP-17.pdf) and a slide show called "Bullying 101: Guide for Middle and High School Students," which includes slides for bullies, victims of bullying, and bystanders (www.pacer.org/publications/bullypdf/BP-28.pdf).

Remember, the point of texture texts is to juxtapose various forms of communication to engage students more critically in the subject matter. This is the perfect opportunity to have students read and talk not only about the information presented in the texture texts, but also about how the information is presented: visually, poetically, through charts and graphs, through eyewitness accounts, through short videos, by explaining statistics, and more. The large number of available texts and text types can assist teachers in differentiating their instruction for the range of readers in their class. And the varied formats can help all students find interesting entry points into the subject matter. Given the amount of context and texture texts to choose from, teachers have many options for enriching the discussion of *Thirteen Reasons Why* in ways that will fulfill college- and career-ready standards and, hopefully, engage more students in the process. Far from undermining the study of literature, using informational texts purposefully can greatly enhance students' exploration of literary texts.

CONCLUSION

Informational texts are indeed texts of power. They bring data, history, real-world knowledge and events, and more to the rich literary experiences that students already have in most English language arts classes. While increased attention to informational texts has disturbed, even shaken, some veteran teachers, we hope this chapter discussion has eased your mind. Informational text does not usurp or put literary text in a backseat. Informational text can work as an enhancement and a partner, and its power can be harnessed to help make fiction, prose, and poetry even more vital and relevant to students.

CHAPTER 6

Social Media Informational Texts: "Electrifying" the Classroom

What is interesting is the power and the impact of social media. . . .
So we must try to use social media in a good way.

—Malala Yousafzai

When we were in high school—and probably you, too—there was a fixed set of genres, and later, when we became teachers, we knew pretty well which of them we should teach. There were lots of places to turn to for definitive information about how these genres worked and what their features were. That world is gone. It slipped away while you were checking your email.

Now, through the "wonders of electricity"—in the form of the Internet, portable devices, and engaging apps—new genres of text, visuals, and combinations of text and visuals, some that even use sound and motion, are emerging at unprecedented rates. If these were radical, underground genres that had no impact on the real world, we could simply ignore them, claiming they aren't the kind of genres we address in English class or in school. But we can't. The world's literacy has been, in a word we borrow from rhetoric scholar Kathleen E. Welch, *electrified*, and it's time we electrify our classroom literacy practices as well.

SOCIAL MEDIA AS INFORMATIONAL TEXTS

These texts and their authors (frequently anonymous) gain readers and viewers by the millions, and often in shockingly short spans of time. Texts, emails, Facebook status updates, tweets, Instagram posts, GIFs (condensed animated and static images), memes (like the ones at the opening of this chapter), blogs, vlogs (video blogs), infographics, Pinterest boards, social bookmarks, and other genres pop up everywhere, and some of these discourses are having a dramatic effect on the world around us. Social media is a popularity contest, and the cool kids—for better or worse—have amazing reach. If you found this list of social media genres dizzying, you might find Tom Zarecki's blog *Social Media's Six Genres* helpful; see https://hubpages.com/education/socialmediagenres.

We do know of good and smart teachers who would prefer that this new world just go away. And we also know of teachers who are creative in avoiding social media and all its attendant aspects. But we think this is a lost opportunity and, indeed, an intellectual and pedagogical stance that benefits no one. As Nobel Laureate Malala Yousafzai points out in the opening epigraph, social media has power and impact; we must do our part to ensure that our students learn to use it "in a good way." Rather than shying away from these new social media genres, we urge you, as a veteran teacher, to confront them head-on by welcoming them into your classroom as valid text types, ripe for the same kinds of critical analysis and discussion we expend on the literary canon.

Ken recently taught a seminar for new college students with that goal specifically in mind.

MANY YOUNG PEOPLE *are heavily engaged in social media. For these digital natives, social media genres have always been there. Even if some forms are taking on sudden importance—for example, who couldn't be awed (in one direction or another) by Donald Trump's use of Twitter?—for today's students, social media genres are ho-hum, nothing new. But young people don't necessarily have the critical literacy skills to understand how social media influences their thinking and changes their worldview and the world's view of them. So I created a course that would focus on the language of social media (specifically examining memes, tweets, and blogs), and I aimed our examinations at texts having to do with social justice, something else that engages many young people today.*

In this chapter, we explore ways to bring new social media genres into your classroom. We start by suggesting one possible method and using that method to explore memes. We then use different methods for examining tweets and blogs. The methods we suggest are options, and they may be applied to many forms of text, particularly emerging text types—for who knows what new genres lie ahead of us in the next few years? (Will there be a critical literacy for communicating with artificially intelligent devices? Will there be conventions for holographic conversations? Is a special genre going to emerge that occurs when conversations occur among passengers in driverless vehicles?) We are intellectually excited by the evolution of electronic genres, and want you, as an accomplished and veteran teacher, to share that enthusiasm and to encourage it in your students.

CRITICALLY EXAMINING EMERGING SOCIAL MEDIA INFORMATIONAL TEXT TYPES

It may seem counterintuitive and even wrongheaded, but we believe that the first thing you must do to help your students develop real critical literacy of new genres is to give up on the idea of your own expertise. We're entering Plato territory here, where the wisest people are comfortable with the fact that they really know very little. You probably have intuited that there are few if any agreed-upon conventions in social media genres, as they are invented and reinvented constantly. So we ask you to truly give up on the idea that you can become an expert on them. Instead, we ask that you become an *expert investigator* of social media genres; that's already in your veteran teacher bag of tricks, and all you need to do is dig in that bag and start pulling some good stuff out.

How can you do this? There's a relatively simple approach you can take to engage students in investigations of emerging social media genres and even of established informational text types. The strategy is to co-conduct empirical studies (examinations of real-world phenomena) with students. Steps in an empirical genre study include the following activities:

1. Gather examples (data)
2. Identify common features in the examples (genre analysis)
3. Generalize rules about the genre (hypothesis)
4. Test the rules with new examples (experimentation)
5. Create your own examples (replication)
6. Study the results of your examples (analysis of findings)
7. Revise your examples (improved hypothesis)

By taking on any of these steps (or all of them), you can join your students as co-investigators of the fascinating world of information and information sharing that surrounds us. And, as an added benefit, you can do so in ways that fulfill many requirements of college- and career-readiness standards.

In the following sections, we demonstrate aspects of this process by applying them to three emerging social media genres: memes, tweets, and blogs. We also explain how this method can be applied to more traditional forms of informational texts.

EXAMINING MEMES

The word *meme* refers to an aspect of a culture or system that is passed from person to person in a way other than genetically. It can be a story, a rule, a convention, and it comes from the idea of "mimesis," an ancient Greek rhetorical concept related to imitation and representation. *Internet memes* are those pictures with text that often go viral and are copied, mimicked, and shared via social media. Although they may seem relatively new, Mike Godwin identified the first *Internet meme* in a *Wired* magazine article almost twenty-five years ago (*Wired* Staff). Godwin found memes in heated Internet conversations, not photos. His most famous find is the "Nazi-comparison meme," about which he codified Godwin's Law: the longer an Internet discussion continues, the more likely it is that someone or something will be compared to Hitler or Nazis. (Anyone who's had a heated discussion about grammar is certainly familiar with this dynamic.) As he witnessed textual memes taking on more currency and power via the Internet, Godwin also described them as *viral*. Fast-forward a couple of decades and add some impressive new technology for sharing pictures and text that depend on shared understandings for their meaning, and you get today's Internet memes, such as these memes about teaching:

Memes are not generally about weighty topics, but they are incredibly effective in spreading information, much of which is implied, which also creates and strengthens bonds among like-minded people. Memes use images, tones, words, and commonplaces (shared understandings) in a manner that carries a significant amount of information with remarkable efficiency and with the eager cooperation of many readers and sharers. Thus, memes are an important genre for all literate citizens to critically understand.

GATHER EXAMPLES (DATA)

Finding examples of memes is easy. Just do an Internet search for "memes" or, if you want to focus on a theme, search "memes about [insert your theme]." (Be warned, memes, like many Internet genres, can be rough: profanity, misogyny, racism, and other unpleasantness and controversy may appear. In fact, in some memes, controversy is a central element or textual feature.)

Once you select a meme, it's a good idea to find at least two more meme examples so that students have several to compare. This makes it easier to identify common features of memes. It's also a smart idea to ask students to find memes they think are especially effective; just be clear about what *you* consider to be school appropriate. On the other hand, we are mindful that students are seeing many controversial memes on their own social media feeds, so we advocate not being too cautious. In Ken's home state, the New York State Common Core Learning Standards also recognize that studying real-world informational texts may require students to work with controversial texts, and referring to that policy may give teachers some cover. Use New York's policy (or a similar policy in your own state) to stiffen your spine when selecting memes to study. Then again, veteran English teachers' spines are already made of the toughest material on Earth!

IDENTIFY COMMON FEATURES IN THE EXAMPLES (GENRE ANALYSIS)

Before asking students to explore the common features of a genre, it's important to help students understand what "common features" in a text such as a meme could be. In other words, we must know what rhetorical appeals are possible in a meme. If memes are intended to get readers to think or do something, what are "the available means of persuasion" in a meme (with a nod to Aristotle)? Or, more colloquially, when we make claims about a meme, what kinds of things can we talk about?

Ken's students came up with these ideas:

- Famous people or characters
- Background image(s)
- Body language of those portrayed
- Facial expression of those portrayed
- Intended audience and other audiences
- Tone of the text
- Facts
- Allusions
- Who is being represented
- Prior knowledge needed
- Diction
- Other images or symbols
- Time frame/recent events (context)
- Use of stereotypes
- Other rhetorical appeals (logical, emotional, and ethical)

The point here is to get students to list as many possible rhetorical features of memes that they can discuss, and then examine what makes a meme effective or not. In addition, it's important to give students some technical language to enable their discussions about textual features of memes. For social media genres, we encourage giving students information about possible "layers of text." The chart in Figure 6.1 shows how Ken shares this concept with his class.

Layers of Text: Analyzing a text means breaking it down to understand how the text makes meaning for readers. A textual analysis is a matter of informed opinion. A really smart textual analysis builds logically on the parts of a text and makes reference to other texts to build a case about what the text means and how it uses other texts and readers' assumptions to make that meaning. There are good and not-so-good textual analyses, but there is not just one, correct textual analysis. There can be a range of interesting and useful textual analyses of the same text.

Text:	The text is all the words, images, colors, and other forms of information that are visible. The text is what is literally on the page/meme.
Context:	The set of circumstances or facts that surround a particular text. The situation in which the text is intended to make meaning. For a meme, this would be the event or events that a meme is intended to respond to. For many memes, current events or pop culture are required knowledge for understanding the meme. Because memes have such vast reach, they can be powerful cultural objects, marking insiders and outsiders and serving as community builders (for better or worse).
Pretext:	Something that is put forward to conceal a true purpose or object; an ostensible reason or excuse. In a meme, a pretext may be a surface reason for making a point, when really the point is about something else entirely.
Subtext:	The subtext is the unspoken or less obvious meaning or message in a text. The subtext comes to be known by the reader or audience over time (not right away), as it is not immediately or purposefully revealed by the text itself. A meme may be about something that many viewers may not even realize unless they have a full understanding of the text and context.
Intertext:	Intertext is when one text refers or builds on the meaning made from another text. Often that secondary text is not explained, but the reader is assumed to understand the reference.
Star Text:	Many memes draw on a particular celebrity (or star) or famous fictional character. These people are not neutral, but instead they come with a whole set of meanings for those who know them. We borrow the term *star text* from film studies to refer to those meanings that a star or a character brings with them to a meme. When a meme becomes a viral genre, the celebrity or character takes on a specific set of meanings in memes that include him or her that need not be explained. The character always speaks in specific phrases, or always connotes a specific tone or feeling. For example, there are Ryan Gosling memes that always start with "Hey Girl," and then say something supportive or romantic, often in a silly way.[1] Memes featuring Laurence Fishburne as the character Morpheus from *The Matrix* always begin with "What if I told you . . . ," which is an allusion to the film. [1]http://www.eonline.com/news/794276/the-oral-history-of-memes-where-did-hey-girl-come-from

FIGURE 6.1. "Layers of Text," a worksheet from Ken's class.

GENERALIZE RULES ABOUT MEMES (HYPOTHESIS)

The next step is to ask students to make their own claims about what something needs to do or include in order to count as an Internet meme. This list could go on for many pages and become more and more formal. In fact, rules for some genres become so formalized that they are codified in manuals, such as the *MLA Handbook* for writers of research papers (now in its eighth edition) or the *Chicago Manual of Style* (in its seventeenth edition). (Note that even codified genres are codified by multiple, competing authorities.) But formal codification is not the goal here. The goal for students is to identify for themselves what the textual features of a good meme seem to be. It's not possible to achieve a single, authoritative list, so every list is a hypothesis, an educated guess based on observation.

Here are some possible textual features of memes students might identify (and this is just a small sample):

- Memes must include a background image; something well known is preferred.
- Especially if the background image is a well-known meme image, memes must follow the set of guidelines that go along with that image.
- Words must appear on the image.
- Sarcasm is common.
- Memes must make a claim, assert a specific viewpoint, or make a pointed critique.

TEST THE RULES WITH NEW EXAMPLES (EXPERIMENTATION)

To strengthen the value of the list of general rules, it's a good idea to ask students to bring in more meme examples, and to try to find some that break the rules. As we know from other aspects of English, excellent creative discourses often break rules, but they break them in a way that creates deeper meaning, not confusion. If your students find a lot of memes that don't follow the rules they have written, they might want to revise the rules they've generalized. This is a form of testing a hypothesis, and it's an important part of genre study.

CREATE YOUR OWN EXAMPLES (REPLICATION) OR ANALYZE AN EXAMPLE USING THE RULES

At this point, you have a choice: keep your students focused on analysis or move them on to composition. Either is appropriate, and your choice simply depends on the goal of your lesson and which standards you have chosen to emphasize.

The assignment that follows actually requires students to do both (note that some meme generators lend themselves to controversy, so check them out yourself before suggesting them to students). For more advice on writing memes with students, check out Traci Gardner's blog post "Making Memes to Illustrate Readings."

Compose, Create, and Analyze Your Own Social Justice Meme

For this assignment, you should create a meme that is intended to convince an audience to take some form of action to support or to oppose something related to social justice. There is a LOT of freedom in terms of choice of topic. Anything that you consider a valuable social-justice-related topic is acceptable.

As you **compose and create your meme**, keep in mind all the many features of memes we have studied in class so far. These should remind you of things you can add to your meme and things you can analyze in your meme:

- The many features of memes that exist
- The layers of rhetorical context available
- The value of deductive rhetoric in the form of an enthymeme
- The use or avoidance of logical fallacies

To create your meme, you may use any of the following, or another meme generator of your choice:

- https://memegenerator.net/

- These were suggested by fellow students:
  - PicsArt (app)
  - GroupMe (app)
  - Kik (app)

Memes are often controversial, even deliberately offensive (at least to some) by nature. Don't shy away from this, but please make every attempt to be thoughtful and responsible. If you have a question about this at all, please feel free to run any idea by me.

Your **meme analysis** should be 500–750 words, and should carefully unpack many aspects of how the meme makes meaning. Just as you used the meme features above to compose your meme, you should use them to analyze your meme as well. Don't be surprised if in your analysis you unpack features that you did not deliberately intend in your meme. (Isn't art fun that way?)

STUDY THE RESULTS OF YOUR EXAMPLES OR ANALYSIS AND REVISE YOUR EXAMPLES (IMPROVED HYPOTHESIS)

Studying the results of a meme (or any other text) is done best through authentic means—i.e., by publishing it to a real audience and getting feedback from that real audience. But results may also come from peers, in a writing workshop, or feedback from a teacher. In this case, Ken invited students to send their memes into the world if they wished to do so, but he required them to submit them to him along with their analyses for a grade. To demystify the grading process, and to help students focus their efforts, he also passed out a scoring rubric (see Figure 6.2). You'll note it includes a bit of snark, which was appropriate for the topic of memes and Ken's students' humor; even with this thick-skinned crowd, however, Ken provided a disclaimer. Oddly enough, Ken's students all claimed they wanted to get the "pile of poo" emoji (http://emojipedia.org/pile-of-poo/) and threatened to do deliberately poor work. (We guess we get the students we deserve!). Ken said he would not give anyone that grade no matter how poorly they did. The threat appeared to have worked, as the students all did quite well.

Revising examples to improve them is an optional step, in the same vein as revising a paper. The purpose here would be to give students the opportunity, as writers, to use feedback to improve their meme. It's how real writers often work, especially regarding informational texts.

Meme and Analysis Scoring Rubric

Visual Quality of the meme: use of images, color, background, etc.					 *
Textual Quality of the meme: use of logic, clever wordplay, smart phrasing, allusions to culture, appropriate attention to conventions, etc.					
Use of analytical vocabulary and concepts in analysis of the meme.					
Cleverness of the analysis of the meme.					
Creativity in the meme and in the analysis.					

* Please note that this column is really a joke. I would never call a student's work !

FIGURE 6.2. "Meme and Analysis Scoring Rubric" from Ken's class.

UNDERSTAND THE POWER OF MEMES

Individual Internet memes may be trivial, but the genre itself can greatly influence people's views. Having understood and agreed with a meme is an active psychological process that has had an impact on a reader's brain. Clicking a Like or a Share button adds a physical engagement that further empowers the community-building power of a meme. As noted before, memes can encourage racism, misogyny, xenophobia—but they can also spread enlightenment, positivity, and logical reasoning. Their power is not yet fully understood, and may never be, but it's clear that building students' critical literacy of memes is not optional. You, that veteran teacher working toward the next level, have an obligation to address this powerful genre.

EXAMINING TWEETS

Tweets are 140-character texts shared via the social media platform Twitter. Readers can like, retweet (share), and reply to tweets, and tweets may include links, photos, and videos. Tweets may also include hashtags (such as #nctechat), which allow users to engage in Twitter chats on specific topics or find other tweets related to the topic. NCTE's Twitter chats back to 2013 are archived here: www.ncte.org/community/nctechat. (For an extremely comprehensive list of Twitter chats related to education, see sites.google.com/site/twitter educationchats/education-chat-calendar). As of April 2017, Twitter had 328 million users, which makes it only the ninth largest social media platform in the world (Sparks). Facebook is the largest social media platform with close to 2 billion users (Sparks). Twitter is different from Facebook in that it limits each message to 140 characters, making one's Twitter feed a quick scroll. Two other platforms, Snapchat and Instagram, are similar (and seem at this point in time to be more regularly used by young people than Twitter), but they emphasize the sharing of photos. Snapchat posts disappear for good after ten seconds, which has prompted significant concerns about cyberbullying. (See http://cyberbullying.org/teaching-snapchat-safety-to-teens for more on the relationship between Snapchat and cyberbullying.) Because of Twitter's increasing popularity and its impact on the professional and adult world, it's appropriate for us to help students learn to navigate this genre. They will almost certainly have to in the future.

Thanks to its chats and an increasing number of professional participants, Twitter has become an excellent platform for professional development in many fields, especially education. But it has also provided space for negativity as well. As Julia Greenberg notes in her "Short History of Twitter":

> People rightfully complain that the platform can be a hotbed for hostility. It also offers a loudspeaker for the disenfranchised, but swarms of voices also silence through harassment[;] . . . it's the world's biggest cocktail party. That means sometimes it's a mess.
>
> But for all its problems, Twitter is everywhere. It's the place where the world talks to itself, often sharing and even making news in the process. Twitter has become a powerful force. . . .

Greenberg's article is a great, quick read. It explores the growth of the platform's influence from its inception in 2006 to 2016, ending with a tweet from Twitter's now most famous (or infamous) user (more on that later). Twitter was the first to break the news of a plane landing in the Hudson River (by Captain "Sully" Sullenberger in 2009); was instrumental in the Arab Spring revolution; provided the first hints of the impending death of Osama bin Laden; and made a powerful organizing tool for the Occupy Wall Street movement (Greenberg).

In the earlier section on memes, we used the format of an empirical study to engage students in meme analysis. We take a different methodological approach to Twitter. In this section, we employ the case study method, examining very closely one tweeter's use of the medium.

A CASE STUDY IN TWITTER: DONALD TRUMP AND WHY WE SHOULD EXAMINE HIS TWEETS

Interest in the influence of Twitter has virtually exploded since Republican Party candidate Donald Trump used it so successfully in his bid to become president of the United States and continued to use it in his presidency.

Regardless of political stance, virtually all agree that Donald Trump's use of Twitter was massively effective and significant in his rise to political prominence. In specific, Trump's style and actions successfully broke many long-standing conventions of running for political office, and his frequent and effective use of the 140-character tweet, in which Trump almost never includes a link, has now piqued the interest of language scholars.

Examining how Trump has used Twitter can be a valuable case study for students to better understand how this new genre can be used to influence debate in a variety of areas. Whereas in our study of memes we demonstrate a genre study approach, here we suggest a case study approach, which means that rather than examining tweets across Twitter, we focus on the many tweets of one individual and the impact of those tweets. In truth, a genre study or case study approach can work for any medium; we simply use a case study here as an example. You and your students may want to look at Trump's tweets as we do, or you might apply this approach to the tweets of some other prominent figure. The advantage of studying Trump's tweets is that so many language scholars have often weighed in on them.

Donald Trump and his tweets were the topic of a case study done by Ken and his students, and Leila and a colleague did a recent presentation for classroom teachers featuring the "Potent Tweet" of both Donald Trump and his opponent Democratic Party candidate Hillary Clinton. But before we explore the details of those, a word on politics in your classroom.

ENGAGING POLITICAL TOPICS IN THE CLASSROOM

Before we start this analysis, perhaps it's important to address an elephant in the room (on the page?): talking about political topics in English classrooms. Once you and your students enter into the arena of social media, it's difficult to avoid controversial, sensitive, and overtly political topics. In a way—and this may be encouraging to you—bringing social media into your discussions makes it far easier to keep your classroom relevant to your students. Because, frankly, in the world of social media, there is no place to hide, and that could be a good thing. While perhaps you would like for much of the controversy and dissention that social media engenders and highlights to go away, it's our belief that it's crucial for you, as an accomplished English teacher, to help your students engage with the material. This teaching is up-to-the-minute, squarely centered in the real world, and we know it is as difficult as any work you do with students. Further, we know that bringing political debate and controversy into your classroom can be challenging. Doing so in a manner that is academic and open requires even greater skill and confidence. And, of course, it's important that you ensure a variety of responsible positions and analyses are not only allowed but also deliberately brought into class discussion.

It's up to each teacher to decide what he or she believes is professionally appropriate. We believe—always—that student learning is paramount, and that if teachers keep that as their primary goal, they can negotiate murky political waters effectively. If there is a policy in your school about such issues, be sure to follow it, but try to push against it if it's too restrictive and you can do so effectively. This is tricky territory for educators, but you're a veteran teacher. You want a relevant classroom. You want students to grapple with some of the most effective and prevalent of language platforms, and you'll find these in social media. You can do this. And we believe you really should do this.

When you take up potentially sensitive—and relevant—topics, it's a good idea to make explicit the purposes of your instruction. Recently, Leila did just that at a professional conference.

THIS PAST FALL A *colleague and I went to our state NCTE affiliate conference, and, for the Virginia Association of Teachers of English (VATE), we presented what both of us saw as a great opportunity for English teachers. Our talk was "Words, Myths, and Wordsmiths: Using the 2016 Presidential Election to Examine Language and Rhetorical Devices" (Christenbury with Gorlewski). Our research had been great fun, and during the presentation, we put the tweets, political slogans, and name calling of both candidates in context, using traditional*

> *sources of language study (classic Greek rhetorical concepts; the famous George Orwell essay "Politics and the English Language"; and study of advertising language and persuasive techniques). What we advocated was treating the almost daily deluge of hot topic/hot button election-related communications as sources for language study, not only enhancing students' analytic skills but also bringing into the English classroom what was occurring on a daily basis. Our selling point to our audience was direct: your class should not have to be hijacked into a forum for pro-Clinton or pro-Trump factions, but it can be a place where the language of both candidates, characterized by exaggerations, distortions, and outright manipulations, is examined and discussed. If we can agree that there are no angels in this arena, the tweets, slogans, and name calling of the 2016 presidential election become fair game for general—and rigorous—examination.*

In his course on the language of social justice, Ken similarly contextualized contemporary politics by including the following in his syllabus:

> Please note that this is a class about the LANGUAGE of social justice. Our work will be focused on ANALYSIS and UNDERSTANDING OF HUMAN COMMUNICATION more than about furthering any specific social justice projects. The goal of the class is for students to better understand how people use language (including written, oral, and visual discourse) to make meaning.

Whether to engage with political discourse in the English classroom is, of course, your choice to make. If ultimately you decide to avoid any politically sensitive topics, you should also understand that you are probably abdicating at least some of your responsibility as a literacy educator. In a democracy, it's crucial that citizens develop critical thinking skills and learn to apply them appropriately to their decisions. There may be no more important area in a democracy than the way language is used—and misused—in political debate about contemporary issues. (See Thompson for an up-to-date look at the language of politics.) Returning to George Orwell, the *Writer's Almanac* notes that Orwell believed there were four great motives for writing prose: sheer egoism, aesthetic enthusiasm, historical impulse, and political purpose. By *political* he meant in the widest sense of the word: "Desire to push the world in a certain direction, to alter other people's idea of the kind of society that they should strive after. Once again, no book is genuinely free from political bias. The opinion that art should have nothing to do with politics is itself a political attitude." But you need to walk this tightrope by using your own rhetorical skills, picking your battles, employing effective pedagogies and best practices, and harnessing your resources (including the advice of colleagues).

ANALYSTS ON DONALD TRUMP'S TWEETS

In a smart and rhetorical theory–informed analysis, Amanda Hess, a David Carr Fellow at the *New York Times*, wrote a 2016 article for *Slate* presciently titled "How Trump Wins Twitter." Hess points to several recurring attributes in then-candidate Trump's tweets, including the following list (all sample tweets are Trump quoted in Hess). See also that some of the bullets are illustrated by the numbered (and superscript) tweets following:

- Inclusion of three to four separate points in a single tweet;[1]
- Using a tweet as a "real-time message tester" and a way to "hone his rhetorical jabs";
- Expressing pity for rivals rather than aggrandizing them as ambitious or powerful (for example, many of his tweets end with "Sad!");
- Leaving out specifics to avoid getting attached to a particular political stance or being accused of making a particular claim; for example, using the ambiguous phrase "certain people";[2]
- Using synonyms to appear to add evidence to a claim without actually doing so;[3]
- Creating an assumed consensus about his own knowledge, opinions, or influence;[4]

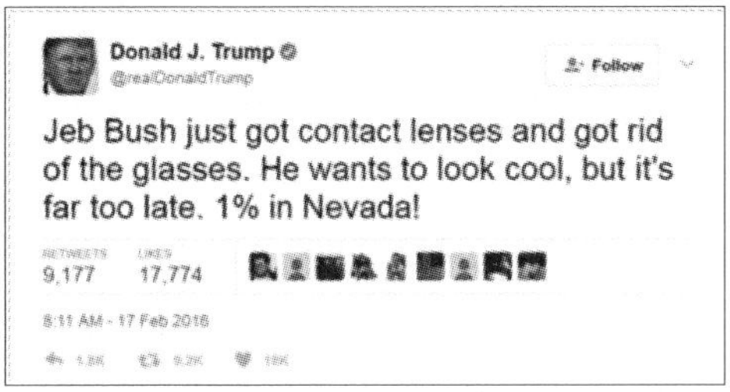

1

2

3

4

One of the key points to note is the number of Likes and Retweets Trump's tweets regularly enjoy. The numbers embedded in these tweets occurred when Trump had 6.23 million followers. As another reporter noted, even back in 2015, Trump used his Twitter account "like a digital native" to "create a community of ever-growing people who appear to agree with him wholeheartedly" (Phillips). At the writing of this sentence, @realdonaldtrump has 33.6 million followers and has sent more than 40,000 tweets. (Although it appears nearly half of those followers may be fake [Bort]). Not all of Trump's followers agree with him, but some of them do, and Trump has direct access even to those who don't. Again, regardless of your political beliefs, this is nothing less than a highly enviable prospect for anyone seeking attention.

Retired University of California, Berkeley, linguist George Lakoff has examined Trump's use of Twitter over several years. He said after Trump was president for several months, "He is a super salesman, and he knows how to change your brain and use it to his advantage" (qtd. in D. White 2017). Trump uses what Lakoff has called "framing" in a variety of effective ways that cause readers (and hearers) to understand him in ways favorable to him and his ideas. Lakoff composed a simple chart (see Figure 6.3) and promulgated it widely via Twitter in which he explains four ways that Trump uses Twitter: Preemptive Framing, Diversion, Deflection, and as a Trial Balloon.

Lakoff's most highly regarded book, with coauthor Mark Johnson, is *Metaphors We Live By*, so it's no surprise that he applies use of metaphor to Trump as well.

> "It is a myth that the truth will set us free," Lakoff said. Case in point: Hillary Clinton's well-thought-out policy positions vs. Donald Trump's tweets. The tweets had one central and fact-free message: "Make America great again." Clinton's message was more detailed and fact-based, but also much more diffuse. Heavy on Enlightenment, short on metaphor. (D. White 2017)

Evan Puschak, aka nerdwriter1, is a popular YouTube poster, and he produced an excellent video titled "A Linguistic Analysis of Donald Trump's Tweets." In his easy-to-follow seven-minute video, Puschak describes, with references to specific tweets, how Trump's use of Twitter shows him "using and manipulating language." Trump's tweets are especially effective as "emotional framing," claims Puschak: "He doesn't want a sympathetic reader

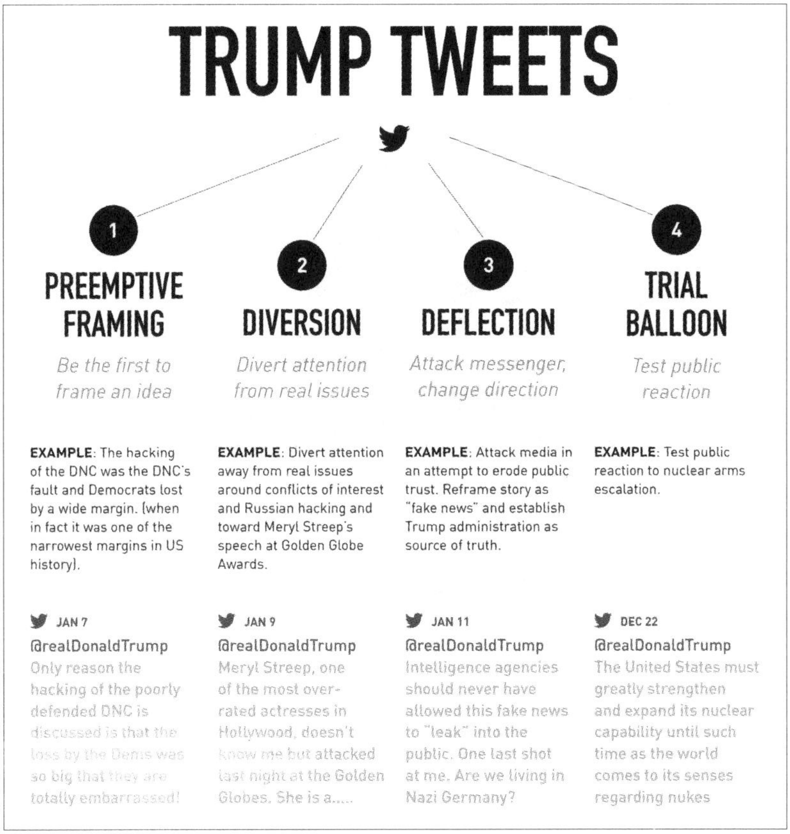

FIGURE 6.3. "Trump Tweets": Created and posted to Twitter by linguist George Lakoff.

to spend any time at all deciphering how to feel about what he's saying." Many of Trump's tweets end with an exclamation, such as *Sad!* or *Ridiculous!*, or *SO WEAK!* Puschak finds these endings are "powerful framing devices that lubricate the content of his message."

Leila and her colleague studied some of the tweets of Trump's rival, Hillary Clinton. While Clinton announced it was her intention not to retaliate (she borrowed a phrase from then First Lady Michelle Obama, "When they go low, we go high"), as the election neared she issued several tweets that took on more of a Trumpian style, such as:

Hillary Clinton
@HillaryClinton
Follow
A person who implies that veterans suffering from PTS are not "strong" is unfit to be Commander-in-Chief. Period.
Donald Trump says, "I love the vets." His record shows otherwise.
Lying about donating to veterans' charities is just the beginning.
hillaryclinton.com
RETWEETS 4,111
LIKES 9,095
7:36 PM - 3 Oct 2016

Hillary Clinton
@HillaryClinton
Follow
Three pages of Trump's tax returns confirm he's a business failure who's gotten rich at your expense. Imagine what he's hiding in the rest.
The New York Times
Trump Tax Records Obtained by The Times Reveal He Could Have Avoided Paying Taxes for Nearly Two Decades
0:33
RETWEETS 15,586
LIKES 28,712
6:36 PM - 2 Oct 2016

Looking closely at both sets of tweets, we can see that Clinton's don't deliver the same impact, at least not with the same people Trump's tweets speak to. She often links to longer statements that explain and lend evidence to her point. She doesn't call names. She doesn't frame as effectively. And she makes one complicated point once, whereas Trump's tweets more often make the same uncomplicated assertion several times.

With the benefit of hindsight, we think Trump's Twitter style did not work for Clinton. Some may argue that Trump took the low road; others may say Clinton "showed up to a gunfight with only a knife." Our stance is simply that Trump's tweets worked more effectively, perhaps demonstrating his clearer understanding of the rhetorical opportunities Twitter makes available. When one should take advantage of such opportunities, if ever, is an ethical dilemma to discuss with your students.

The point of focusing on Donald Trump's tweets is not simply to elevate one person's tweets for analysis—many members of the American political, economic, and entertainment establishment are now tweeting more than ever—but it's also to point out what rich rhetorical material there is in just 140 characters. As important as classical rhetoric and contemporary communications are to fully understanding how argument works, the time we spend in class discussing enthymemes, syllogisms, or logical fallacies can be dry with theory. Using tweets to fuel relevant and real-world analyses of contemporary debates in social media genres can engage even the most reluctant learners among our students. This is where language study becomes alive and up-to-the-minute. And, while in this chapter we have no middle-level or high school classroom vignette to share on this topic, we are hopeful that as the semesters roll on, we will be in classrooms where students and their teachers examine and discuss such powerful communication tools as Twitter.

BEYOND DONALD TRUMP: TWITTER CHATS AND TWITTER ANALYTICS

Although here we focused on a single tweeter, there is much more to explore about Twitter. Doing a search on Twitter can reveal interesting information about limitless topics and people. And you can use Twitter to have a Twitter chat about Twitter, using a specific hashtag for your class chat. (A hashtag is a word or phrase preceded by the pound sign, such as #nctechat.) A great feature of the hashtag is that people need not follow one another to engage in a chat on Twitter. Ken has an explicit social media policy in which he states that he will not knowingly follow his students; he has to say "knowingly" because users can create anonymous accounts. But it's still important for everyone to know that unless one sets one's privacy settings very deliberately, everything on Twitter is entirely public and will be available for as long as the Internet exists.

Ken engaged his class in a Twitter chat that focused on three simple questions about Twitter as a platform for social justice issues, each question delivered every couple of days over the course of a week:

- What are some positive aspects of Twitter for social justice? Please retweet examples of tweets that show your point.

- What are some negative aspects of Twitter for social justice? Please retweet examples of tweets that show your point.
- Is Twitter a net positive or a net negative for social justice?

In their answers to the questions, students retweeted interesting tweets, gave brief analyses of what they found, and replied back and forth to one another about their opinions. At the time, Ken was surprised that none of his students had previously participated in a Twitter chat, even though most of them had accounts and owned smartphones. (This is another lesson about the importance of not assuming our students are social media experts; it also confirms that young people use social media differently from adults.)

Another interesting thing that happens in Twitter chats is that other users can simply butt in (unless you make a chat private). In Ken's class, this was welcome, because most of the uninvited guests were colleagues. If a guest causes trouble, it's a simple matter to block them. And it's not difficult to create private Twitter chats or to use an alternative platform, such as TodaysMeet.

If you haven't yet heard about data analytics, you soon will—and they're much more interesting when they're not about test scores. Twitter analytics can tell you about the reach of your own tweets. Figure 6.4 displays the set of Twitter analytics from a tweet Ken made of a blog that lists good YA texts. Let's look at this chart. On the left is Ken's tweet, and on the right is a list of analytics. First on the list, *impressions* are the number of people who scrolled through a Twitter feed that included the post; they may not have read it or even seen it, but they had the opportunity to do so. *Engagements* are when the tweet elicited action from a viewer: they may have clicked the link, clicked a button to Like the tweet, retweeted the tweet to their followers, looked at Ken's Twitter feed (to see if he might be someone they'd like to follow), or clicked on the tweet to expand it and examine it further. All social media platforms have analytics programs attached, and big data software, such as Python, can read the data and help marketers, pollsters, and other influencers make evidence-based decisions. These new opportunities are sweeping across all professions, and all future professionals will need a keen understanding of data analytics to be gainfully employed. As an English teacher, you can help your students by introducing them to Twitter analytics early.

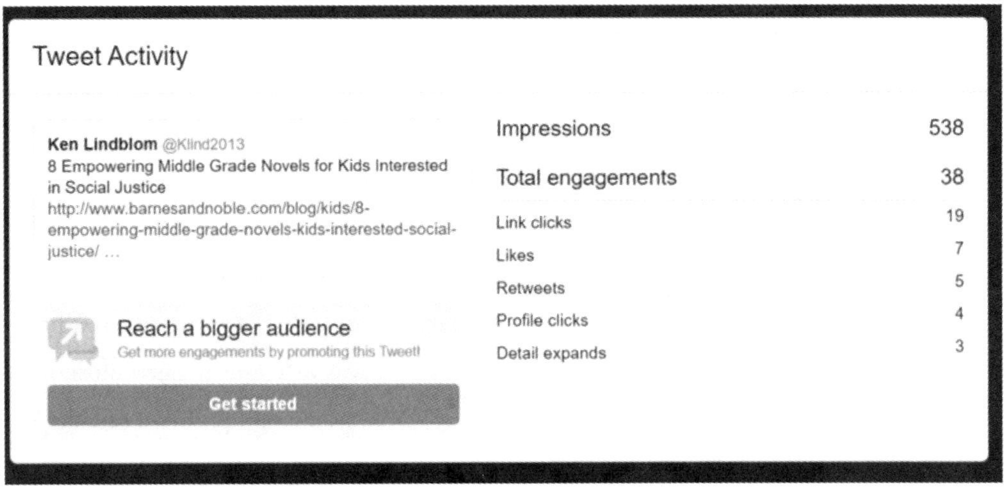

FIGURE 6.4. Twitter analytics from Ken's tweet of a blog listing good YA texts.

Twitter and similar chat platforms can also provide valuable thinking spaces for students and teachers while they are in class together. A quick stop in our ideal Teachers' Lounge brings us to English teacher Nicole Galante, a veteran teacher from Bay Shore High School on Long Island, New York, who is now Ken's colleague at Stony Brook University. A technology whiz, Nicole is tapping away on the newest iPhone model, and in between taps, she tells us how she uses a platform like Twitter to raise the level of discussion in her classes.

FROM THE TEACHERS' LOUNGE

Using TodaysMeet for Back-Channel Conversation

Nicole Galante

Stony Brook University, State University of New York

Technology in the classroom should be used to give students the opportunity to do or create something that otherwise would be impossible using traditional methods. One such opportunity social media can

provide is for a back-channel conversation, *one that takes place digitally and occurs simultaneously with a face-to-face discussion or lecture. This is particularly useful for students who may be hesitant to share their ideas during whole-class discussions, as well as for students whose voices may be suppressed by physical or other disabilities, and to allow for varied processing rates in any given classroom.*

I use the website TodaysMeet (www.todaysmeet.com), a private chatroom, with students during every class so that we can collaborate on note taking, share resources with one another by linking notes in the conversation to YouTube videos or research, participate in guided discussions of texts or active viewing of films together, or even hold "icebreaker" discussions that are opinion-based and can be answered anonymously in the chat room. TodaysMeet does not require a login, can be accessed from any device (including students' smartphones and tablets), and is completely private. It also requires students to be concise—enacting the 140-character limit ubiquitous on social media.

When using TodaysMeet to contain the back-channel conversation, teachers can choose to keep the room active for up to one year and invite remote participation from students who may have to miss school or from parents or other classes. TodaysMeet also provides PDF transcripts, so each conversation can be uploaded to a Google Classroom or class website.

Back-channel conversations have been an integral part of my teaching and learning since I discovered them nearly five years ago. My students and I have been able to participate in collaborative, generative conversations that give all students a voice in a space parallel to traditional learning.

EXAMINING BLOGS

Another social media topic of importance to you and your students is blogs. Most histories of blogs, a shortened version of the term *weblog*, date their inception to the mid- to late 1990s. By the mid-2000s, there were millions of blogs on the Internet. The idea of chronicling one's thoughts or travels goes back to the ancient world, and even further if one includes the oral tradition, but Internet blogs are unique in their reach, because they are easily acquired, read, and shared. Blogs usually have a central theme of some sort, and while they don't generally have the kind of viral speed that tweets or memes have, many of them are read regularly by tens or even hundreds of thousands of readers.

The field of education is host to many great blogs, including *Edutopia* (www.edutopia.org/), Larry Ferlazzo's *Classroom Q & A* blog with teachers (http://blogs.edweek.org/teachers/classroom_qa_with_larry_ferlazzo/), *Talks with Teachers* (http://talkswithteachers.com/), and—of course—*Literacy & NCTE* (http://blogs.ncte.org/), the official blog of NCTE. Among others, there's also a successful blog created by an NCTE subgroup, the Conference on English Education, called *Writers Who Care* (https://writerswhocare.wordpress.com/), one of the first blogs to use a blind peer review process like that of academic journals. All of these are blogs that you would enjoy reading as a veteran English teacher; there are literally thousands on other topics that would interest your students.

Blogs can be created using a variety of easy and free platforms. Our favorite is WordPress because it offers simple directions and a variety of useful features, the blog analytics are impressive, and its for-pay upgrades are worth consideration.

Ken recently asked his students to undertake a genre analysis of blogs, using the assignment sheet in Figure 6.5. Working together, the students came up with a variety of interesting answers, compiled in the following lists:

Blog Rhetorical Analysis

In order to compose (or analyze) an effective blog, one must understand the rhetoric of a blog. Over 2,600 years ago, Aristotle defined rhetoric as "the available means of persuasion." Given this, what are the "available means of persuasion" in a blog? In other words:

What tools does a blog make available to authors to help them convince their readers to think or to do something?

Visual tools:

Textual tools:

Other tools (social tools):

FIGURE 6.5. "Blog Rhetorical Analysis": An assignment from Ken's class.

Visual Tools

- Blog aesthetics
- Colors of words used (can grab attention)
- Pictures
- Memes
- Videos

- Statistics
- Interactive polls/questions
- GIFs that help emphasize a particular point
- Ethnic, gender, socioeconomic class, and other cultural characteristics of people that are most frequently shown in images displayed on the blog
- Use of emojis
- Infographics
- Overall presentation (no one will read something that doesn't look good)

Textual Tools

- Links to related articles or blogs
- Bullet points and numbered lists
- Catchy titles
- Puns
- Different fonts and sizes
- Controversial themes
- Quotes from others
- Rhetorical appeals
- Twitter excerpts
- Italics to emphasize a section or subsection of the blog
- Hashtags that are used within the blog
- Diction/syntax
- Rhetorical questions

- Tone
- Ability to write in other languages

Other Tools (social tools)

- Links to follow on Facebook, Twitter, Instagram, Pinterest, Tumblr, LinkedIn, Google+
- Advertisements related to the topic you're reading about
- "Follow" button
- Space for comments
- Comparing to other blogs
- Sharing buttons at the bottom of blogs
- A comment section to spark a conversation about the material being presented
- Testimonials from other people in the social world who have experience with the topic you're talking about (telling a story)
- SoundCloud (the inclusion of music)
- Surveys/polls about important societal issues related to the blog content
- Collaborating with other organizations that are also credible

Having examined all the possible ways bloggers can use blogging technology to present information effectively and engagingly, students were then given an assignment to either write up a lengthy analysis of a blog or to create a short blog post of their own and then write a brief analysis of it, as outlined on the following page.

Social Justice Blog (Composition) Analysis

Direction: Choose A or B, not both

A. Select a social justice–oriented blog with at least 3 posts. Include a link to the blog and **write a 700–800 word rhetorical analysis** of the blog. In your analysis, be sure to consider many of the "available means of persuasion" that we have discussed in our class during the semester.
B. **Compose a 200–350 word social justice–oriented blog post** (just a single post). You may use any free blog platform to create this. WordPress is recommended. In addition, **write a 350–450 word rhetorical analysis** of the "available means of persuasion" that you used in your blog post.

One of the most interesting aspects of blogs is the use of language. Blogs are often personal. They tend to be written by a single author who is attempting to create an ongoing relationship with readers. The language is often informal, even quirky, and yet the best blogs include links to authoritative resources that enhance the author's credibility. *Ethos, logos, pathos*, and myriad other rhetorical appeals are exploited creatively through words, pictures, sounds, colors, links, author bios, photos, and other means.

Ken writes a blog on education (*edukention*), and his final post of 2016 described the kind of data analytics WordPress provides its authors. It shows the numbers of views, when each view occurred, and from what country they were read. Blog posts are shared by their authors and enthusiastic readers who share their links on Twitter, Facebook, and their own blogs, as well as on other social media platforms. Although his success is modest even by education blog terms, Ken's blog still reaches more than 4,000 people and has been read in forty countries. Clearly, blogs have an impact, and students should learn to read and compose them critically.

Performing a genre analysis of blogs in English class is an excellent way to engage students in critical examinations of a limitless number of topics while also focusing on the language (broadly defined) that is at work in a blog. Although we don't discuss video blogs here, your students may also be interested in analyzing what are now called "vlogs."

And these forms of technology, especially Twitter and blogs, involve writing. Veteran teacher Jocelyn A. Chadwick reminds us:

> I often hear colleagues say students don't write. Of course they do! Students today write far more than many of us "back in the day." Their writing also contains beginning, middle, and end; audience, occasion, purpose. While their writing does not look traditional, we can learn from their many modes and venues of expression. We must remember, there is no one way to write. Leveraging their modes situates them to entertain and learn from us other forms of writing. (personal communication, 2017)

CONCLUSION

When social media first emerged and then rapidly became a potent and widespread source of communication, most schools and their English teachers were careful to draw boundaries around its use in the classroom. For a few years, "instant messaging" or "IMing" (now called "texting") in particular was seen as encouraging a deterioration of proper language skills, and sharing on platforms such as Facebook was similarly viewed as alarming and even disruptive to good order in the classroom. (At the time, Leila was interviewed by almost two dozen regional and national news organizations whose reporters almost always wanted her to agree that the abbreviations and argot of texting was on its way to permanently marring young people's use of language. Leila never saw it that way, and it didn't really happen, did it?) Many adults treated these electric genres as though they were truly dangerous, as though the wires could deliver terrible shocks and devastating burns (which isn't entirely untrue, metaphorically). School policies enforced this concern, and some well-meaning, even forward thinking teachers were cautioned and even disciplined for using social media more liberally in their teaching and with their students. At the time, discussing the skills needed to create a static website or craft a professionally standard email was considered acceptable and even safe; the ever-changing and morphing forms of social media, however, were more the territory of the Wild West and something to be avoided in school.

Of course, this is nothing new. Technology, especially technology that captivates the young, is usually, historically, met with suspicion and its use often linked to the charge of moral baseness. Just as Plato railed against the technology of writing for making young men lazy and insolent, so teachers in the early 2000s complained about texting and Myspace.

Today, social media is a worldwide force. Global communication has truly become electrified. You, as an accomplished teacher, know the power of social media in your students' lives—as well as locally, in your own life and even in the lives of your older relatives and friends who use it daily and with many positive effects. We use social media for an amazing range of purposes from the historic to the mundane: to gather at Tahrir Square, to spread the word about terrorist attacks or coup attempts, to broadcast "pop up" gatherings, to share the latest gossip or joke, to apologize to our mothers, to ask our partners if we need to pick up more milk.

As we continue to teach responsibly and well, to uphold standards of clear and honest communication, to read with our students the best of classic and contemporary literature, we must also open the door to the world of social media, to engage our students' electrified literacy skills and practices and to help them understand and make decisions about how it is used—and misused. Such teaching is vibrant and energized, and—as your students will note—relevant and forward-thinking. This is another manifestation of what we wrote about in a previous chapter: faring forward; faring, actually, into today and the near future as we help our students and ourselves negotiate today's rich and complex world of communication. It is our obligation. It is our privilege. It is one aspect of English language arts that drinks deeply of everything today can bring.

CHAPTER 7

What Veteran Teachers Tell Us

Effective teaching requires more. More time. More planning.
More researching. More knowledge and understanding of the people
who sit in your classroom.

—Kara Greenwood, Patrick Henry High School

Our new "captains" have never been at the helm of a classroom
and are every bit as mad as any Ahab. Teachers now find themselves
in the untenable position of standing on the beach screaming "SHARK,"
while the world merrily dives into the surf.

—Jennifer Menzel, Hampton High School

I suspect another reason I have lasted so long in the classroom is because
I am never, ever bored. The intense drama of adolescents in high school is endlessly fascinating, rewarding,
and demanding.

—Clary W. Carleton, Open High School

We believe that those who have spent much of their professional lives in the classroom and remain professionally engaged have garnered along the way understanding and even wisdom. We trust this does not sound pretentious or imply that mere hours logged in a classroom always result in improved teaching and superior insight. But, in fact, if you are one of those who after some years are still teaching and still enthusiastic about your teaching, you have developed both knowledge and judgment. You have also earned our deep respect for what you know and you practice every day. We all can learn from you.

To put it mildly, veteran teachers have not generally been shown appropriate respect in the media, among politicians, or among various other groups who have, as we are all aware, various motives. Representations of teachers in film and television almost always distort the real knowledge and labor that good teaching requires, and we guarantee that anyone who thinks teachers, with summers off, ride their ways to easy pensions has never actually taught. These views are simply wrong. As colleagues of many dedicated, smart, and accomplished classroom teachers, we can attest to the quality and strength veteran teachers exhibit every day over countless hours in countless schools. We seek to honor this.

It seems appropriate, then, that we make significant space in this book for the voices of veteran teachers, people who have for some years worked well with students and negotiated successfully the many pitfalls and challenges of daily teaching, of school systems, and of changing requirements. We invited a number of veteran teachers to write about what they might offer to others from their positions as experts, and their responses fall into three areas: *insights*, *cautions*, and *encouragement*. All of these can be helpful to us, and we detail them in the following sections.

These colleagues' experiences and insights extend our ideal Teachers' Lounge, bringing more hard-won wisdom from the field to this text.

INSIGHTS

Hampton High School veteran teacher Sierra Ware recalls the old and well-worn advice about being "mean" during the first few months of teaching, aka the Don't-Smile-until-Christmas approach. Not surprisingly, it didn't work for her (it also didn't work for Leila or Ken, neither of whom is good at holding back a guffaw, never mind a smile). Sierra's advice, as she learned to reject what was not a fit, is to "be true to yourself," as she also has learned to be in her years of teaching. For Sierra, that sense of being true extends to her whole teaching philosophy: "The more honest you are in your teaching, the better the classroom culture. A great classroom culture encourages the students to take the risk necessary to grow academically and socially." Making bridges to her students ("always remember that the kids need you!") is also essential, and, for Sierra, within her classroom that has meant "incorporating the students' likes and dislikes and letting students know you have commonalities." A shared endeavor is positive and generative.

For Midlothian Middle School veteran Katherine Byers, teaching success is twofold—mentoring and learning from your students:

> I believe being a part of mentor relationships is the key to continuous, successful learning and teaching. Every person has something to teach me. For this reason, I am open to learning from my students, peers, and administrators alike. I also prioritize mentoring students, especially those who are considered "difficult" or "high risk." My commitment to the students that are seen as troublesome has shown me that those are often the ones who have the most need for support and guidance. Through strong personal relationships, I am able to excite a high level of engagement from my students because they know I earnestly believe each and every one matters.

In Katherine's case, this kind of commitment has other benefits in that it often, she feels, is apparent to others and has an almost contagious effect:

> The passion to grow as an individual and encourage that same passion for self-improvement in students is at the heart of my professional ethic. People notice when a person is open to learning from others and doesn't shy away from challenging relationships. Being open to mentorship is being open to learning, listening, and results in effective communication and strong relationships.

Kelly Ann Pace is a veteran at Patrick Henry High School, a recognized Teacher of the Year in her school and school district, and, when she was dealing with students who didn't appear to value each other, she intervened in the following way, and it has had long-term consequences for her and her teaching. This is the story she tells:

> I asked my students to take out a piece of paper, write their name on it, and pass it to their left. They were then asked to write for two minutes on the paper that was passed to them. The topic? Nothing that related to English. . . . I asked them to write what they admire, what they like, what inspires them about that person whose paper they had in front of them. They had two minutes.
>
> The room was silent as my students furiously wrote. After two minutes, they passed their papers to the left again. This went on until they had their original paper in front of them, and the bell rang.
>
> This was, by far, the best lesson I have taught in my nineteen-year teaching career. It originated as a means to correct some mean behavior I had witnessed among my students and students outside of my classroom. The actions were small things—like not holding the door for someone on crutches or excluding others in conversations. While seemingly miniscule examples of destructive behavior, they began to take a toll on me, and I decided to do something to rectify these actions. There was no traditional English lesson that day, no literature discussed, no literary devices analyzed, no thesis statements drafted. Yet, what happened in my classroom that day is something that as a teacher, I will remember for a long time to come: my students felt valued.
>
> Since that day, I have attempted to be a teacher who values her students. A good teacher doesn't stand in front of her students, but behind them—in what they do, in who they are, in how they act, in what they learn. Good teachers build relationships. Instead of being frustrated by unengaged students, I find a solution. I listen to my students. I get to know their personalities. I show them I care—every single day. I make them feel valued. Good teaching means not being afraid to make mistakes but rather to embrace them and learn from them. The circle writing exercise that day could have completely backfired. Luckily, it did not, and my students left feeling empowered.

That day, Kelly and her students experienced the power of community writing and of writing that is truly meaningful to students and to her. It was driven by an authentic need—to increase empathy among students—and it resulted in a powerful community of writers.

For Clary W. Carleton, the multiple variables of teaching inform how she thinks about her students and her classroom:

> A seemingly infinite number of variables impact learning, but only some are in the teacher's control. Teaching is therefore humbling and hard. For me, it is also exciting, messy, and relentless—class after class, day after day, year after year. It is emotionally, even physically draining, but I nonetheless have extraordinary days inspired by the real human drama of teaching and learning. It is a vocation where the well-being of others is connected to my own. I care deeply about my students because they connect me to something bigger than myself.

Clary's comments remind us how ill-informed many education reformers are, as they claim (or imply) that a quality teacher will transform students' lives and upend wide-scale poverty and other forms of inequity. That said, she also points out some of the genuine joys of teaching, the pleasure that comes from the generative chaos, the pride that comes from doing truly good work for young people who deserve it, the deep and restful sleep that comes from working with others.

Clary's insights are probably ones you identify with.

INSIGHTS TO REMEMBER

We appreciate and will remember these insights our colleagues have shared:

- Don't shy away from your true personality in the classroom. Students, by their nature, will test your boundaries, and they will find them. There's no need for you to create and present an artificially mean personality to manage a classroom effectively.
- Try to learn something new from each student. Doing so will encourage you to respect and to see the best in each student.

- Take risks to create real community among your students. You will actually be teaching them the skills and knowledge that come from the English language arts.
- Remember that teachers are human. Many things are out of your control, and you can only change the things in your power to change. And what you can control may be enough.

CAUTIONS

Some hard-won insights of many experienced teachers are also serious words of concern and even caution. Kara Greenwood reminds us:

> Effective teaching is not easy. Anybody can slap some worksheets together and give them to students and call it teaching . . . effective teaching requires more. More time. More planning. More researching. More knowledge and understanding of the people who sit in your classroom. More learning.
>
> I remember being a new teacher thinking that it would be easier after a few years. I thought I wouldn't have to "reinvent the wheel" every year. Once I taught a particular course, I thought I would have notes and plans and lessons so the next year would be easier. The reality is, though, that my students are not the same every year and that in order to meet their needs, I have to find new strategies and activities to keep them engaged and interested in learning. After all, that's what it's all about. Students learning.
>
> I teach students, not courses, and in order for learning to occur, I, the teacher, have to be willing to learn.

Jennifer Menzel had a fairly rough introduction to teaching, but she found her footing, and she shares her story as well as a realistic assessment of how a veteran views teaching today:

> "We're going to need a bigger boat."
>
> This was my predominant thought at the end of my first day as a teacher. Granted, the start of my career was unorthodox. I was hired in mid-January of

> 2003. The person I was replacing had gone on the holiday break with the grade book, a stack of assignments, and had not returned. As a result, I inherited a roving schedule of 11th and 12th grade English classes. At the door of the first class, I was informed they were "Somewhere in *Macbeth.*" This was, of course, the one big-gun tragedy by Shakespeare I had not read. The kids were unruly after two weeks of substitute teachers. The seniors were frantically angry over the loss of their grades. By the end of that day, all I could picture was that scene from *Jaws* where the audience finally sees the shark.
>
> Still, I stuck with it. That was fourteen years ago, the early, halcyon years of NCLB, before testing became the prescribed course. Now, as new species of sea monsters circle, they take the forms of data-driven education, Secretary of Education Betsy DeVos, state-regulated graduation quotas, and testing corporations offering computer-generated poetry. Our new "captains" have never been at the helm of a classroom and are every bit as mad as any Ahab. Teachers now find themselves in the untenable position of standing on the beach screaming "SHARK," while the world merrily dives into the surf. Seems a bit overblown, doesn't it? Not really.
>
> Please, don't get me wrong. I still love teaching. The actual teaching part, that is. But overall, I am deeply disillusioned. Education has been sold to the sharks of capitalism, under a façade of quality assurance and safety in the numbers. Meanwhile, educators know that real learning doesn't happen under quotas, data is not truth, and that our "boats" are only going to get smaller.

One of the issues many English teachers struggle with is relevance and making a case to our students that what we are doing in the classroom has a connection to their lives. For veteran teacher Marie Gist of Midlothian Middle School, this concern is not insurmountable:

> Everything you do in the classroom matters. When planning, focus on the things that you can control. Think about SWBATs or any of the million student-centered planning acronyms you have been inundated with over the years. At the center

> of all of this jargon is the student. . . . What do you need to be successful? When I plan, I think about what I want them to learn from the lesson itself and how this experience will inform future learning and deepen their understanding of the world around them. This is no small task. Teaching commas can seem very dry, but the gift of the ELA teacher is that we wear all hats. We are thinkers, dreamers, and masters of interconnectivity. Give yourself pause. Open your mind. Wait. You will find the relevance.

Finally, Clary W. Carleton writes about the contract good teachers have with their students and about the ways this contract can be exhausting and yet nonnegotiable:

> I must prove my worth each day at a pace that might surprise non-educators. Adolescents demand honesty and authenticity. Like Holden Caulfield, they can spot a phony, and without a well-established filter, they tell you what they think. At the secondary level, teachers must therefore withstand constant evaluation and feedback in real time. But I ask students to trust me, and I must reciprocate. This takes courage and stamina. Stamina is also required when administrative measurement of learning and worship of big data seem to overshadow the learning itself.

While some of these cautions may seem negative to you, they are also realistic assessments of the many challenges teachers face today. As experienced classroom instructors, we have in some ways seen it all—or something much like it. Acknowledging that and trying to deal with it positively is part of the challenge of the veteran teacher.

CAUTIONS TO REMEMBER

Veteran teachers share worthy cautions we should all keep in mind:

- Don't fall in love with your old lessons. Your students change, and they will learn better if your lessons are adapted for them.

- Keep your focus on the students. The myriad political and bureaucratic distractions these days in education can be dizzying. Let your work with your students be your center.
- Young people are eager to learn what they will need in order to be successful, happy adults. Everything you can to do help your students understand the relevance of your teaching will help to engage them.
- Be real and be strong. Your students will appreciate you as a flawed person if you act authentically and acknowledge the pressures you face, even as you stand against them for the good of your students.

Let's take a walk over to our Teachers' Lounge. Today we find Lisa Scherff, a classroom teacher with a truly unusual journey. She began her career as a ninth- and tenth-grade ELA teacher, went on to become a professor at several universities, and then left the university-level to teach high school full-time again. Lisa was also coeditor of NCTE's *English Education*, a journal for and about developing middle and secondary school ELA teachers.

FROM THE TEACHERS' LOUNGE

What I've Learned Going Back to the Classroom

Lisa Scherff
Cypress Lake High School, Fort Myers, Florida

As an ELA teacher for twenty years, I have experienced the increasingly negative influence of external assessments, which have negatively impacted the curriculum, and what I have learned is this:

- *The prevalence of testing in its most recent iteration has created a double whammy in classrooms: Because of the narrow focus on close reading, oftentimes fewer texts in total are read (and these texts are often short or excerpts), causing a narrowing of the curriculum, which then results in less focus on or consideration of students' background knowledge and creates disengagement and apathy. Ironically, this then creates additional problems for students' wider reading, background knowledge, motivation, and achievement (even on assessments). The conundrum is how to give background knowledge necessary to help students do well on mandated tests, how to provide them with the necessary literacy "practices" (thanks, Judith Green, for the term practices over skills) to be successful in life, and how to inspire a love of reading and writing.*

- *I have learned that it is hard. As a "veteran" teacher/teacher educator who returned to the classroom in 2013, I lost my once-earned tenure. Like all other new teachers in Florida, I am on an annual contract, which means at any time I can be pink-slipped. This can create pressure on many teachers to toe the line and implement harmful pedagogical practices. It can cause them to abandon independent reading, teaching full-length works, incorporating research, and many other essential literacy practices and experiences.*
- *I have learned that today's students—just like those I first taught in 1996—want to read widely, want to investigate and discuss political and social issues, want to read novels and plays, and want to write about things they care about. If we are not careful and do not resist harmful mandates, these passions might disappear.*

And then we can spend every day "close reading."

ENCOURAGEMENT

For Kelly Ann Pace, as for many veteran teachers, there are real and definable rewards to teaching. She shares:

> The rewards in teaching are not tangible, financial, nor quantitative. Rewards lie in the student who suddenly understands exactly what I've been talking about for the past eighty-five minutes. Rewards lie in the student who tells me that his mind has been blown away by what the class just discussed (as he puts the tips of his fingers to his temples, imitating an explosion). Rewards lie in the student who tells me that she couldn't put down the book that we are reading. Rewards lie in the student who returns to my classroom six years later to thank me because he never did that when he was in high school. Rewards come in that same student telling me that I made a difference.
>
> So what have I learned as a veteran teacher? I've learned that effective teachers empower their students to see their self-worth. Effective teachers enable their students to feel valued. And most importantly, I've learned that teaching is not just about content but about showing the students who they truly are. It is only then that as a teacher I have been able to learn who I am.

For Clary W. Carleton, the classroom itself remains lively and engaging, and she believes that that dynamic has kept her interested and positive:

> I suspect another reason I have lasted so long in the classroom is because I am never, ever bored. The intense drama of adolescents in high school is endlessly fascinating, rewarding, and demanding. Also, some things do get easier. For example, I have a much better sense of what will and will not work in the classroom. I am more willing to take risks because I am confident that I can defend my practice. I am also less likely to crumble when a lesson fails since I now know this is inevitable and a reflection of my own willingness to try new things.

ENCOURAGEMENT TO REMEMBER

Veteran teachers are the best people to offer one another a few words of encouragement:

- Celebrate every lightbulb moment you see in your students, every bit of new understanding. We teachers live for these moments. Enjoy them fully.
- Remember that the good you do may not show up for years to come, but it will make a true difference in real lives.
- Enjoy the confidence and strength your students show: you helped build that.
- Revel in your world: Students are endlessly entertaining and interesting. You may be exhausted, but you're never bored.
- Feel confident in your abilities. You have made it as a teacher to veteran status. Few have and even fewer could. You're pretty damned good at what you do.

CONCLUSION: CONTINUING THE JOURNEY

Teaching is a journey. The road of a teacher is rarely smooth, often dotted with potholes and scattered with bumps. Unexpected wildlife leaps into the middle of that road without warning, and we meet more than a few memorable characters along the way, including some we'd prefer to avoid. The road is long and arduous, and it can be lonely. Leila and Ken write together in part because it's more fun sometimes to walk with a friend, and good friends accept us for all our flaws and mistakes. They appreciate and applaud our attempts. And the journey, taken well, never really ends. For there will be colleagues ready to continue it when we're done walking, and we can rest, knowing we've done our part and more.

Because you've been reading this book, chances are you are also one who understands the joys and challenges of the teaching journey. And, like the best teachers, you have probably learned that there is always more for you to learn, that despite every fall or stumble, you will learn from the experience and teach again. Good teaching makes us humble. Veteran teacher Dave Stuart Jr. puts it well:

> The humble teacher is able to objectively analyze her performance, be it in classroom management or instructional design or gradebook upkeep. She aggressively seeks to learn from her failures. He keeps close tabs on how he's doing . . . because few things are of greater use to others than the work of a never-finished, always-growing educator.

Teaching is unique in that the longer you do it, the more you know you have so much left to learn. It's not easy to continue this journey, but it's worth the effort. Every blister, every sprained ankle, every aching muscle is a reminder of how many miles we've come and how many lives we've touched along the way. For this reason especially we keep walking. We continue the journey.

WORKS CITED

Alim, H. Samy, and Django Paris. "What Is Culturally Sustaining Pedagogy and Why Does It Matter?" *Culturally Sustaining Pedagogies: Teaching and Learning for Justice in a Changing World,* edited by Django Paris and H. Samy Alim, Teachers College Press, 2017, pp. 1–21.

Alsup, Janet. *A Case for Teaching Literature in the Secondary School: Why Reading Fiction Matters in an Age of Scientific Objectivity and Standardization.* Routledge, 2015.

Alvarez, Deborah. Post in "Teaching and Learning Forum." National Council of Teachers of English Connected Community, 8 Mar. 2017.

Anderson, Mike. *The Well-Balanced Teacher: How to Work Smarter and Stay Sane inside the Classroom and Out.* ASCD, 2010.

Asher, Jay. *Thirteen Reasons Why.* Penguin Random House, 2007.

Beers, Kylene, and Robert E. Probst. *Reading Nonfiction: Notice & Note Stances, Signposts, and Strategies.* Heinemann, 2016.

Berk, Brett. "Brash. Vulgar. Extinct. The Creation and Demise of GM's Hummer." *Autoweek,* 10 July 2017, pp. 11–13.

Blunt, Judy. *Breaking Clean.* Knopf, 2002.

Bort, Ryan. "Nearly Half of Donald Trump's Twitter Followers Are Fake Accounts and Bots." *Newsweek,* 30 May 2017, www.newsweek.com/donald-trump-twitter-followers-fake-617873.

Boser, Ulrich. "Teacher Diversity Revisited: A New State-by-State Analysis." Americanprogress.org, May 2014, https://cdn.americanprogress.org/wp-content/uploads/2014/05/TeacherDiversity.pdf.

Bradway, Becky, and Doug Hesse. *Creating Nonfiction: A Guide and Anthology.* Bedford St. Martin's, 2009.

Brown, Brené. "The Power of Vulnerability." TED Talk, 3 Jan. 2011 (TED.com).

Burrus, Daniel. Quotefancy, https://quotefancy.com/quote/1716198/Daniel-Burrus-Information-is-power-only-if-you-can-take-action-with-it-Then-and-only-then.

Chadwick, Jocelyn A. "We Dare Not Teach What We Know We Must: The Importance of Difficult Conversations." *English Journal, vol.* 106, no.2, Nov. 2016, pp. 88–91.

Chadwick, Jocelyn A., and John Grassie. *Teaching Literature in the Context of Literacy Instruction.* Heinemann, 2015.

Charlton, James I. *Nothing about Us without Us: Disability Oppression and Empowerment.* U of California P, 2000.

Chartook, Jonas, and Weiner, Ross. "How to Save Teachers from Burning Out, Dropping Out and Other Hazards of Experience." *The Hechinger Report,* 13 Nov. 2014, http://hechingerreport.org/content/can-keep-great-teachrs-engaged-effective-settele-careers_18026/.

Chicago Manual of Style. 17th ed. U of Chicago P, 2017.

Christenbury, Leila. "From the Editor." Focus Issue: Veteran Teachers: The Challenge of the Long Distance Runner. *English Journal,* vol. 85, no. 5, 1996, pp. 11–12.

———. "Race Differences: A White Teacher and a Native Son." *Oops: What We Learn When Our Teaching Fails,* edited by Brenda Miller Power and Ruth Shagoury Hubbard, Stenhouse, 1996, pp. 77–81.

———. *Retracing the Journey: Teaching and Learning in an American High School.* Teachers College Press, 2007.

Christenbury, Leila, with Julie A. Gorlewski. "Words, Myths, and Wordsmiths: Using the 2016 Presidential Election to Examine Language and Rhetorical Devices." Virginia Association of Teachers of English Annual Conference, Newport News, 2016.

Christenbury, Leila, and Ken Lindblom. *Making the Journey: Being and Becoming a Teacher of English Language Arts.* 4th ed., Heinemann, 2016.

CNN/ORC International Poll. "Interviews with 1,012 Adult Americans Conducted by Telephone by ORC International on September 4–8, 2015." CNN/ORC International, 13 Sept. 2015, http://i2.cdn.turner.com/cnn/2015/images/09/12/iranpoll.pdf.

Cortez-Riggio, Kim-Marie. "The Green Footprint Project: How Middle School Students Inspired Their Community and Raised Their Self-Worth." *English Journal,* vol. 100, no. 3, pp. 39–43.

Couros, George. *The Innovator's Mindset: Empower Learning, Unleash Talent, and Lead a Culture of Creativity*. San Diego, Dave Burgess Consulting, 2015.

Dickinson, Emily. "1286. There is no Frigate like a book." 1873. *The Poems of Emily Dickinson,* edited by R. W. Franklin, Harvard UP, 1999.

Draper, Sharon M. *Not Quite Burned Out but Crispy around the Edges: Inspiration, Laughter, and Encouragement for Teachers.* Heinemann, 2001.

Dunn, Patricia A. *Disabling Characters: Representations of Disability in Young Adult Literature.* Peter Lang, 2015.

———, guest editor. Re-Seeing (Dis)Ability. *English Journal* [Special Issue], vol. 100, no. 2, Nov. 2010.

———. *Talking, Sketching, Moving: Multiple Literacies in the Teaching of Writing.* Heinemann, Boynton/Cook, 2001.

El-Bermawy, Mostafa M. "Your Filter Bubble Is Destroying Democracy." *Wired*, 18 May 2016, www.wired.com/2016/11/filter-bubble-destroying-democracy/.

Eliot, T. S. *The Dry Salvages [Four Quarters]. The Complete Poems and Plays 1909–1950*. Harcourt Brace & World, 1952.

Emba, Christine. "Cultural Appropriation Is a Problem. A Misguided Burrito Cart Is Not Part of It." *Washington Post,* 2 June 2017.

Fletcher, Ralph. *Making Nonfiction from Scratch.* Stenhouse, 2015.

Gallagher, Kelly. *Readicide: How Schools Are Killing Reading and What You Can Do about It.* Stenhouse, 2009.

Gardner, Traci. "Making Memes to Illustrate Readings." *Bedford Bits,* 1 Jan. 2017, https://community.macmillan.com/community/the-english-community/bedford-bits/blog/2017/01/24/making-memes-to-illustrate-readings.

Garner, Bryan A. *Garner's Modern American Usage: The Authority on Grammar, Usage, and Style.* 3rd ed., Oxford UP, 2009.

Gilyard, Keith. *Voices of the Self: A Study of Language Competence.* Wayne State UP, 1991.

Gorlewski, Julie, and David Gorlewski. 2016. "Editors' Introduction to Special Section: Teaching *Adventures of Huckleberry Finn:* Essays in Conversation." *English Journal,* vol. 106, no. 2, 2016, p. 74.

Greenberg, Julia. "On Its 10th Birthday, a Short History of Twitter in Tweets." *Wired,* 21 Mar. 2016, www.wired.com/2016/03/10th-birthday-short-history-twitter-tweets/.

Hallman, Heidi L. "Authentic, Dialogic Writing: The Case of a Letter to the Editor." *English Journal,* vol. 98, no. 5, May 2009, pp. 43–47.

Harter, Amy E. "The Joy Stays Consistent." *NCTE Centennial Website: "Then and Now,"* 2011, www.ncte.org/centennial/teacherstories/amyharter. Reprinted 13 Mar, 2011, on www.universeastext.com by Amy E. Casey (née Harter).

Haynes, Mariana. "On the Path to Equity: Improving the Effectiveness of Beginning Teachers." *Alliance for Excellent Education,* 17 July 2014, www.all4ed.org/reports-factsheets/path-to-equity/.

Hess, Amanda. "How Trump Wins Twitter." *Slate,* 13 Feb. 2016, www.slate.com/articles/technology/future_tense/2016/02/donald_trump_is_the_best_at_twitter_here_s_why.html.

Hesse, Douglas. "Imagining a Place for Creative Nonfiction." *English Journal,* vol. 99, no. 2, Nov. 2009, pp. 18–24.

Hoaglund, Edward. "What I Think, What I Am." *New York Times Book Review*, 27 June 1976.

Ingersoll, Richard M. "Beginning Teacher Induction: What the Data Tell Us." *Education Week,* 16 May 2012, www.edweek.org/ew/articles/2012/05/16/kappan_ingersoll.h31.html?tkn.

James, William. *Pragmatism and Other Writings.* Penguin, 2000.

Jaschik, Scott. "Analyzing Black Lives Matter without Black People Involved." *Inside Higher Ed*, 30 May 2017, https://www.insidehighered.com/news/2017/05/30/philosophy-journal-apologizes-symposium-black-lives-matter-written-without-black.

Jewett, Michelle. "Whitesplaining the Canon." *English Journal*, vol. 106, no. 5, May 2017, pp. 93–96.

Kafele, Baruti K. *The Teacher 50: Critical Questions for Inspiring Classroom Excellence.* ASCD, 2016.

Kirkland, David E. *A Search Past Silence: The Literacy of Young Black Men.* Teachers College Press, 2013.

Kynard, Carmen. *Vernacular Insurrections: Race, Black Protest, and the New Century in Composition-Literacies Studies.* State U of New York P, 2013.

Lakoff, George, and Mark Johnson. *Metaphors We Live By.* Chicago UP, 1980.

Lindblom, Ken, et al. "Composing Infographics to Synthesize Informational and Literary Texts." *English Journal*, vol. 105, no. 6, July 2016, pp. 37–45.

Lorde, Audre. "History Is a Weapon: The Master's Tools Will Never Dismantle the Master's House." 1979, www.historyisaweapon.com/defcon1/lordedismantle.html.

Lutz, William. *Doublespeak: From "Revenue Enhancement" to "Terminal Living": How Government, Business, Advertisers, and Others Use Language to Deceive You.* Harper & Row, 1989.

Mack, Nancy. "Energy and Enthusiasm: Don't Start the School Year without Them." *English Journal*, vol. 98, no. 1, Sept. 2008, pp. 18–25.

McCann, Thomas M., Larry R. Johannessen, and Bernard P. Ricca. *Supporting Beginning English Teachers: Research and Implications for Teacher Induction.* National Council of Teachers of English, 2005.

Miller, sj, editor. *Teaching, Affirming, and Recognizing Trans* and Gender Creative Youth: A Queer Literacy Framework*. Palgrave Macmillan, 2016.

Modern Language Association. *MLA Handbook*. 8th ed., MLA, 2016.

Morris, Sarah L. "Helping Students Learn." *NCTE Centennial Website: "Then and Now,"* 2011, http://www.ncte.org/centennial/teacherstories/sarahmorris.

National Council of Teachers of English. *Teachers, Profs, Parents: Writers Who Care.* Conference on English Education blog, NCTE, 2017, https://writerswhocare.wordpress.com/.

Newkirk, Thomas. *Minds Made for Stories: How We Really Read and Write Informational and Persuasive Texts.* Heinemann, 2014.

Nieto, Sonia. *What Keeps Teachers Going?* Teachers College Press, 2003.

Orwell, George. "Politics and the English Language." *Shooting an Elephant, and Other Essays*. Secker and Warburg, 1950.

———. "Why I Write." *A Collection of Essays*. 1946. Harvest Harcourt Brace Jovanovich, 1981, pp. 309–16.

Palmer, Parker J. *The Courage to Teach: Exploring the Inner Landscape of a Teacher's Life.* Tenth anniversary ed., Wiley, 2007.

Pang, Alex Soojung-Kim. *Rest: Why You Get More Done When You Work Less.* Basic Books, 2016.

Pariser, Eli. "Beware Online 'Filter Bubbles.'" TED Talk, March 2011, www.ted.com/talks/eli_pariser_beware_online_filter_bubbles.

Patel, Leigh. "The Irrationality of Antiracist Empathy." *English Journal*, vol. 106, no. 2, Nov. 2016, pp. 81–84.

Pennac, Daniel. *Better Than Life.* Translated by David Homel. York, ME: Stenhouse, 1999.

Phillips, Amber. "The Surprising Genius of Donald Trump's Twitter Account." *The Washington Post*, 10 Dec. 2015, www.washingtonpost.com/news/the-fix/wp/2015/12/10/reading-6000-of-his-tweets-has-convinced-us-donald-trump-is-a-social-media-master/?utm_term=.5c051198odc2.

Puschak, Evan (nerdwriter1). "A Linguistic Analysis of Donald Trump's Tweets." *Digg*, n.d., http://digg.com/video/how-donald-trump-tweets-sad.

Quintilian. *Institutes of Oratory, or, Education of an Orator*. Translated by John Selby Watson, revised and edited by Lee Honeycutt, 2007, and Curtis Dozier, 2015.

Rankin, Jenny Grant. *First Aid for Teacher Burnout: How You Can Find Peace and Success*. Routledge, 2017.

Ressler, Paula, and Becca Chase, guest editors. Sexual Identity and Gender Variance. *English Journal* [Special Issue], vol. 98, no. 4, Mar. 2009.

Rodríguez, R. Joseph. *Enacting Adolescent Literacies across Communities: Latino/a Scribes and Their Rites.* Lexington Books, 2017.

Roosevelt, Eleanor. *You Learn by Living: Eleven Keys for a More Fulfilling Life.* 1960. Harper Perennial, 2011.

Smagorinsky, Peter. "Huck and Kim: Would Teachers Feel the Same If the Language Were Misogynist?" *English Journal,* vol. 106, no. 2, Nov. 2016, pp. 75–80.

Smith, Michael W., Deborah Appleman, and Jeffrey D. Wilhelm. *Uncommon Core: Where the Authors of the Standards Go Wrong about Instruction—and How You Can Get It Right.* Corwin, 2014.

Solebello, Marlana. Review of *The Arrival,* by Shaun Tan. *English Journal,* vol. 106, no. 5, May, 2017, pp. 80–82.

Solnit, Rebecca. "Occupied Territory." *Harper's,* July 2017, pp. 5–7.

Southworth, Amy Jo. "Poised to Partner: The 21st-Century School Librarian." *English Journal,* vol. 102, no. 5, May 2013, pp. 94–96.

Sparks, Daniel. "How Many Users Does Twitter Have?" *The Motley Fool,* 27 Apr. 2017, www.fool.com/investing/2017/04/27/how-many-users-does-twitter-have.aspx.

Stuart, Dave Jr. "How Humility Makes Us Better, Saner Teachers." *Dave Stuart Jr.,* Apr. 2017, www.davestuartjr.com/sanity-humility/.

Sutcher, Leib, Linda Darling-Hammond, and Desiree Carver-Thomas. "A Coming Crisis in Teaching? Teacher Supply, Demand, and Shortages in the U.S." *Learning Policy Institute,* 15 Sept. 2016, https://learningpolicyinstitute.org/product/coming-crisis-teaching.

Thomas, Angie. *The Hate U Give.* Balzer & Bray, HarperCollins, 2017.

Thomas, Ebony Elizabeth. "Is *Huck Finn* Still Relevant? Revisiting 'The Case for Conflict.'" *English Journal,* vol. 106, no. 2, Nov. 2016, pp. 85–87.

Thompson, Mark. *Enough Said: What's Gone Wrong with the Language of Politics?* St. Martin's Press, 2016.

Twain, Mark. *Following the Equator: A Journey around the World.* 1897. Dover Publications, 1989.

Villanueva, Victor, Jr. *Bootstraps: From an American Academic of Color.* National Council of Teachers of English, 1993.

Walker, Timothy D. "The Disproportionate Stress Plaguing American Teachers." *The Atlantic,* 7 Oct. 2016, https://www.theatlantic.com/education/archive/2016/10/the-disproportionate-stress-plaguing-american-teachers/503219/.

Welch, Kathleen E. "Electrifying Classical Rhetoric: Ancient Media, Modern Technology, and Contemporary Composition." *Journal of Advanced Composition,* vol. 10, no. 1, Jan.–Feb. 1990, pp. 22–38. *JSTOR,* www.jstor.org/stable/20865696.

Wessling, Sarah Brown. "Passion for Learning and Teaching." *NCTE Centennial Website: "Then and Now,"* 2011, www.ncte.org/centennial/teacherstories/sarahwessling.

Wessling, Sarah Brown, with Danielle Lillge and Crystal VanKooten. *Supporting Students in a Time of Core Standards: English Language Arts, Grades 9–12.* National Council of Teachers of English, 2011.

White, Daphne. "Berkeley Author George Lakoff Says, 'Don't Underestimate Trump.'" *Berkeleyside,* 2 May 2017, www.berkeleyside.com/2017/05/02/berkeley-author-george-lakoff-says-dont-underestimate-trump/.

White, E. B. "On a Florida Key." *One Man's Meat.* Harper & Row, 1983, pp. 175–79.

Whitehead, Alfred North. *The Aims of Education and Other Essays.* 1929. The Free Press, 1957.

Wired Staff. "Meme, Counter-Meme." *Wired,* 1 Oct. 1994, www.wired.com/1994/10/godwin-if-2/.

Woolf, Virginia. "From 'The Modern Essay.'" *Essayists on the Essay: Montaigne to Our Time,* edited by Carl H. Klaus and Ned Stuckey-French, U of Iowa P, pp. 44–47.

Wordsworth, William. "Nuns Fret Not." 1807. *The Longman Anthology of Poetry,* compiled by Lynne McMahon and Averill Curdy, Pearson/Longman, 2006.

The Writer's Almanac with Garrison Keillor. "June 25: Birthday: George Orwell." 25 June 2015, https://

writersalmanac.org/note/june-25-birthday-george-orwell/.

Yousafzai, Malala. "25 Malala Yousafzai Quotes That Have Changed the World." *EverydayPower,* compiled by Jeffrey L. Moore, 19 Apr. 2015, https://everydaypowerblog.com/2015/04/19/malala-yousafzai-quotes/.

Zarecki, Tom. "SOCIAL MEDIA's Six Genres." *HubPages,* updated 22 Feb. 2017, https://hubpages.com/education/socialmediagenres.

Zongker, Doug. "Chicken Chicken Chicken: Chicken Chicken." *Annals of Improbable Research,* Sept.–Oct. 2006, www.improbable.com/airchives/paperair/volume12/v12i5/chicken-12-5.pdf.

INDEX

Note: A "t" following a page number indicates a table; an "f" indicates a figure.

AUTHORS

LEILA CHRISTENBURY is Commonwealth Professor of English Education at Virginia Commonwealth University, Richmond, where she has taught English methods, young adult literature, applied English linguistics, and the teaching of writing. A past president of the National Council of Teachers of English (NCTE) and a past editor of *English Journal*, her research has been recognized by the David H. Russell Award, the James N. Britton Award, and the Edward B. Fry Book Award. An active member of NCTE for more than 40 years, she has taught in Virginia high schools and universities for most of her career. She is the author of numerous books, chapters, and articles on the teaching of English, and her personal life is filled with pets, friends, reading, film, and singing soprano in her church choir. She can be contacted at lchriste@vcu.edu.

KEN LINDBLOM is associate professor of English and dean of the School of Professional Development at Stony Brook University, where he teaches courses in English teacher education and rhetoric and leads the university's teacher and leader education programs. A member of NCTE since 1989, Ken was editor of *English Journal* from 2008–2013, and he is currently book review editor for the journal. He is coauthor of two other books about teaching English and more than two dozen articles, book chapters, and peer-reviewed blog posts on the subject. His tenth-grade sense of humor wins him equal numbers of friends and enemies, which is better odds than he deserves. He can be contacted at kenneth.lindblom@stonybrook.edu and @klind2013.

FROM THE TEACHERS' LOUNGE CONTRIBUTORS

VICTORIA ALESSI, a National Board Certified Teacher, will be entering her eighteenth year of teaching this fall. She has been teaching seventh- and eighth-grade English in Smithtown, Long Island, for the past 15 years.

JOCELYN A. CHADWICK, current president of NCTE, has more than 30 years' experience as a teacher, scholar, and author. Spending the first 10 years of her career as a high school English teacher, Chadwick went on to inspire young minds at higher learning institutions in Texas. She recently served as professor of English at Harvard University in the Graduate School of Education and is now a guest lecturer at Harvard. She is also a nationally recognized Mark Twain scholar.

ALEX CORBITT (@Alex_Corbitt) is a seventh-grade English teacher at the Bronx School of Young Leaders. His work focuses on motivation, education technology, and literacy.

LISA STORM FINK works at NCTE in professional learning and also acts as project manager of ReadWriteThink.org. After teaching grades K–4 for almost nine years, she brought her varied experiences full-time to NCTE. Lisa enjoys sharing the site with others during professional development opportunities, as well as with her preservice teachers at the University of Illinois.

NICOLE GALANTE teaches methods, adolescent literature, and non-Western literature at Stony Brook University, where she is also acting director of the English Teacher Education Program. She consults in New York City schools in all five boroughs, training and mentoring teachers and administrators, and building connections between pre- and inservice teachers. From 2008–2013, she worked as an associate editor of *English Journal*, and before that was a classroom English teacher for seven years on Long Island.

KELLY GALLAGHER is a high school English language arts teacher in Anaheim, California, and a popular author and consultant. He's been a leader in several key literacy projects (including the California Reading and Literature Project, the South Basin Writing Project at California State University, Long Beach, and the Puente Project), and he served as President of the Secondary Reading Group of the

International Reading Association. Gallagher's highly regarded books include *Readicide* (2009) and *In the Best Interest of Students* (2011).

DOUG HESSE is professor and executive director of writing at the University of Denver. He was the 2016 president of NCTE, and previously was chair of the Conference on College Composition and Communication and president of the Council of Writing Program Administrators. He publishes frequently about creative nonfiction, including his book *Creating Nonfiction*, with Becky Bradway (2009).

SHARON HINKSON is a second-career English teacher at Longwood Junior High School in Middle Island, New York, where she has taught for five years. Previously, she spent six years in special education as a teaching assistant. She earned a BA and MA in English at Stony Brook University, as well as a BA with a history and economics concentration at St. John's University. Formerly a recruiter and benefits supervisor in the corporate world, followed by many years as a stay-at-home mother to three wonderful children, Hinkson loves movies, reading, and dancing.

SUSAN HOUSER served as president of NCTE in 2017. Previously, she served the Pinellas County (Florida) Schools for 14 years as a teacher of middle school reading, language arts, and gifted language arts, and she was president of the Florida Council of Teachers of English. She received a specialist degree in educational leadership from Argosy University, Tampa. In 2011, Houser was named NCTE Outstanding Middle Level Educator in the Language Arts.

LAUREN LEIGH KELLY taught high school English full-time for 10 years in New York, focusing on curriculum development and teaching for social justice. She developed curriculum for courses in spoken word poetry, hip-hop literature and culture, and theater arts at the school where she also taught tenth- and twelfth-grade English. After earning her PhD from Teacher's College, Columbia University, Kelly received a postdoctoral research fellowship at Boston University's School of Education, and she became an assistant professor at Rutgers University in 2017. She has published in *English Journal* and the *Journal of Adolescent & Adult Literacy*.

PENNY KITTLE is an English teacher and literacy coach at Kennett High School in North Conway, New Hampshire. She teaches tenth, eleventh, and twelfth graders each fall and also occasionally in the alternative night school for adult students. She is also the author of *Book Love: Developing Depth,*

Stamina, and Passion in Adolescent Readers (2012), *Write Beside Them: Risk, Voice, and Clarity in High School Writing* (2008), and a number of other popular books about teaching and writing. Kittle was also a columnist for NCTE's *Voices from the Middle* for six years.

THOMAS NEWKIRK is the author of *Embarrassment: And the Emotional Underlife of Learning* (2017) and numerous other titles, including *Minds Made for Stories* (2014), *The Art of Slow Reading* (2012), *Misreading Masculinity* (2002), and *The Performance of Self in Student Writing* (1997, winner of the NCTE David H. Russell Award). For almost three decades, he taught writing at the University of New Hampshire, where he founded the New Hampshire Literacy Institutes, a summer program for teachers. In addition to working as a teacher, writer, and editor, Newkirk has served as the chair of his local school board.

R. JOSEPH RODRÍGUEZ is a literacy educator and researcher in the Texas Hill Country and San Joaquin Valley of California. He is the author of *Enacting Adolescent Literacies across Communities: Latino/a Scribes and Their Rites* (2017) and several journal articles. He has taught English and Spanish language arts in public schools, community colleges, and universities. His areas of research include children's and young adult literatures, language acquisition, and socially responsible biliteracies. He will serve as coeditor of *English Journal* from 2018 to 2023. Catch him virtually @escribescribe or at rjrodriguez@csufresno.edu.

ANNA J. SMALL ROSEBORO, retired from Calvin College in Grand Rapids, Michigan, is a National Board Certified Teacher who has taught students in grades 7 through graduate school in five states: Missouri, New York, Massachusetts, California, and Michigan. She is past president of the California Association of Teachers of English (2002–04) and currently serves as co-director and mentor for the NCTE Early Career Educator of Color Leadership Award program and co-chair of the Conference on English Education's Commission to Support Early Career English Language Arts Teachers.

After 11 years as a teacher educator, in 2013 **LISA SCHERFF** returned to the high school classroom, where she has taught several courses, such as Pre-AP English, Critical Thinking, Reading, and AP Research. She has been active in NCTE/ALAN for many years, serving as a journal coeditor, chair of the Walden Award, chair of the NCTE Assembly for Research, president of the Alabama Council of Teachers of English, and member of multiple committees. In 2016 Scherff was named Lee County School District's secondary ELA Teacher of the Year.

AMY JO SOUTHWORTH is a school librarian at Mary G. Clarkson Elementary School in Bay Shore, New York. She taught English for 12 years and occasionally teaches composition and technical communication for Stony Brook University.

This book was typeset in Calluna and Saira by Barbara Frazier.
Typefaces used on the cover include Joe Hand 2, Galaxie Polaris, and Gill Sans MT.
The book was printed on 50-lb. White Offset paper by Versa Press, Inc.